You ask what is meant by "breaking
out of humanity." But poetry
can't be translated into prose
without seeming exaggerated and
mystical, or else flattened down
to mere common sense. Either
way gives a false picture. ~~So~~ But
I ~~can only~~ ^{may} suggest several things
that were meant by the one saying.

① We have learned within the past
century or so that humanity is only
a temporary and infinitesimal phenomenon
in a large universe. The knowledge
involves a readjustment _{of values} that can only
be managed by looking at humanity
objectively, from the outside.

② The phrase refers also to those moments
of visionary enlightenment that I should hate
to call "cosmic consciousness" because so
much foolishness has been written about
them under that name.

③ It seems to me wasteful that almost
the whole of human energy is expended
inward, on itself, in loving, hating, governing,

cajoling, amusing, its own members. It is like
a new-born babe, conscious almost exclusively
of its own processes and where its food comes
from. As the child grows up its attention
must be drawn from itself to the more
important world outside it.

④ In a civilization like ours, metropolitanism
intensified by machinery, human nature
(which was developed under very different
conditions) becomes an anachronism.
We can't turn back the civilization, not
at least until it collapses, and our
descendants will have to develop a
new sort of nature — will have to
"break out of humanity" — or suffer
considerably — probably both.

I could specify a good many more ideas
involved in these one phrase, but my
letter mustn't go on forever. Indeed I
am not sure that I've indicated even
now the thoughts that were uppermost in
my mind when I was writing.

                    Robinson Jeffers.

Shine, Perishing Republic

ROBINSON JEFFERS AND THE
TRAGIC SENSE IN MODERN POETRY

by

RUDOLPH GILBERT

HASKELL HOUSE
Publishers of Scholarly Books
NEW YORK
1965

published by

HASKELL HOUSE

Publishers of Scholarly Books

30 East 10th Street • New York, N. Y. 10003

Library of Congress Catalog Card Number:65-15883

PRINTED IN UNITED STATES OF AMERICA

NOTE

THESE essays, it is hoped, will introduce new readers to Robinson Jeffers. A poet of his power sees
with a too complex vision "the spiritual realities to
which the material realities correspond" to be understood by proxy. Only by a daring leap into the midst
of the foaming, resounding storm-waves of his titanic
poems can the reader become sensible of the "divine
vision in time of trouble" of Robinson Jeffers. For he,
like Blake, will never be among our popular poets.
They remain ever the poets of those seekers of the *élan
mystique* in poetry, that quality which is outside its
delicacy or its force, its verbal beauty or its rhythmic
cadence, its lyric song or its tragic cry. The poetry
of a Blake or a Jeffers is marked by too many obscure
figures of speech and too few clear narratives to make a
general appeal. We may emphasize the unpopularity
of Blake, Crane, Jeffers and T. S. Eliot with the
words of Eliot himself: "the genuineness of poetry is
something which we have some warrant for believing
that a small number, but only a small number, of contemporary readers can recognize. I say positively only
a small number, because it seems probable that when
any poet conquers a really large public in his lifetime,
an increasing proportion of his admirers will admire
him for extraneous reasons." Yet to those few who

7

have felt the remote, strange elevation of thought and lonely strength of inhuman agony in the spirit of Blake, the work of Jeffers will offer a spiritual adventure leading by a new path back to the world of imagination where all poetry has its origin.

These essays are written from an inquiring point of view. They supplement from a somewhat new mental angle the numerous reviews, criticisms and essays on Jeffers which have already appeared, and are dedicated to sympathetic readers belonging to that brotherhood which the author of *The City of Dreadful Night* calls "the Open Secret Society of poets and mystics."

A more detailed and critically inclined interpretation of Robinson Jeffers's work may perhaps be forthcoming in the near future, we sincerely hope, from the author of *The Golden Day,* or of *The Modern Temper,* or *Challenge to Defeat.*

Grateful thanks and appreciation are due to Mr. and Mrs. Robinson Jeffers for perusal of the manuscript and encouragement. To M. Webster Brown for invaluable help in the editing, to E. Merrill Root for suggestive criticisms, to Horatio Robert Swasey for his generous and friendly spirit of judgment, to William J. Burke and Francis A. Lynch, members of the New York Public Library staff for bibliographical and detailed information.

R. G.

Briarcliff Manor
    New York

CONTENTS

I. *THE POET OF OUR TIME*

The singers do not beget, only the Poet begets,
The singers are welcom'd, understood, appear
  often enough, but rare has the day been, like-
  wise the spot, of the birth of the maker of
  poems, the Answerer.
                                    Whitman

THE POET OF OUR TIME

ROBINSON JEFFERS has brought "something fiery" into American poetry. Although he is American-born, we sense in him a unity of thought with some of the greatest of the Europeans. In the numerous reviews and criticisms of his work we find Jeffers called overwhelming, electrifying, savagely uncontrolled, burning with incestuous passion. Cestre endows him with "instinct brutal et vision mystique." V. F. Calverton, the class-conscious telamon among the literary critics of the moment, in his book, *The Liberation of American Literature,* writes: "Jeffers's tragedies are a reflection of the violent toppling-ruins of a dying civilization. Never has such desperately dooming poetry been written in this century." Edna St. Vincent Millay has this to say about Jeffers: "People can't understand his sort of poetry because of its terrific implications. It's like seeing enormous mountains for the first time, or the sea—you're terrified by them. Here is a fine poet and a great man, a man that in his own generation will not be known to the public at large." In fact we taste a strong Jeffersean flavor in Millay's latest poetic chalice *Wine from These Grapes* in such lines:

Detestable race, continue to expunge yourself, die out,

.   .   .   .

Put death on the market;
Breed, crowd, encroach, expand, expunge yourself, die out,
Homo called sapiens.

William Hale in his *Challenge to Defeat* writes: "We are in search of the man who goes from introversion to extraversion; the man who starts out with the flaming emotion, the full impression, the deep selfhood—but who does not spend his lifetime in delivering 'a pageant of the bleeding heart.' Robinson Jeffers—although himself a passionate introvert—has said: 'The mind of humanity centered upon itself will go mad'; we must work, that is, from the inward to the outward; from the study of ourselves we must proceed to a study of the world." In the new *Encyclopaedia of the Social Sciences* under "Literature" we read: "In the post-war disintegrative period of modern capitalistic society, with the strong focussing of its contradictions, there has come again an interest in death, represented strikingly by Thomas Mann and Robinson Jeffers; the one looking upon it as a soil from which art and beauty spring, the other looking upon it as the final breaking-through to Reality." H. Seidel Canby in the *Saturday Review of Literature* writes: "Good-natured people go to excess when they feel deeply. In spite of its morbidity, and perhaps because of it, here is a poem *(Give Your Heart to the Hawks)* that troubles the waters as if there passed by some angel of judgment."

Rodolphe Louis Megroz ends his *Modern English Poetry:*—"There is apparently no contemporary English narrative poet whose work can vie in power with the American, Robinson Jeffers."

Let us forget for a moment the reviews and current opinions, favorable and unfavorable, and go back to the transmission of life from one generation to another. At all times and on all sides we behold nature engaged in her ceaseless work of reproduction. The unsolvable mystery of that wondrous creative process of nature manifested in plants, animals and man is as deep in the minds of men as it was in the dawn of the world's history. But in those primitive ages the mighty *élan vital* was conceived as more material, more personal, more closely allied to man himself, until the period of belief in an anthropomorphic god.

To the Greeks the phallic god, Pan, became the supreme procreator. The pagans were beset with terror, in dread of blind cruelty, afflicted with a sense of helplessness. Pagan man was no more than an unregenerate human animal, and Apollonian culture stood for a time chiefly for this pagan man's regeneration. Retreating still farther into antiquity we find the Assyrian trinity of Asshur, Anu and Hoa representing the trinity of the generative organs. The earlier mystery of Isis and Osiris, the Eleusinian mysteries of the Greeks, the mysteries of Venus and of Bacchus at Rome —all these ancient festivals celebrated new-born life and the regenerative union of the creative elements in nature and man. To the ancients the sun was a male symbol; the moon, like the earth, being receptive only, was regarded as female. The crescent moon was an emblem of virginity.

The Old Testament affords numerous examples of holiness attached to the phallic symbol. To lay the hands upon the generative organs of the person to whom a vow or promise was made is referred to in the twenty-fourth chapter of *Genesis:* "Put, I pray thee, thy hand under my thigh." Stones set up for pillars or altars and the pouring of oil upon them are often mentioned in the Bible. The pillar was in fact originally the emblem of a large phallus erected to honor the creator of all life. To the Druids certain kinds of trees possessed a religious and phallic significance. In the animal kingdom the bull to the Egyptians, the cock and the goat to the Greeks, the centaur and the unicorn in the early ages, were symbolic of creative energy and life-giving force.

After these few brief comments on some of the most familiar of the age-old symbols Jeffers uses, we are in a better position to consider and comprehend his attitude toward life as expressed in his poetry. Nature is merciless, beyond good and evil, like Thoreau's "naked

Nature, inhumanly sincere, wasting no thought on man." It is only through transcending our humanity, by becoming inhuman with nature, that we can see and live face to face with God and "not waste inward upon humanity." Humanity has become "something we must break away from."

To questions of our own times is Jeffers "the Answerer." Local surroundings serve him as setting for the cosmic action of his "giants in agony." Just so ancient Greece served Aeschylus and Euripides, who also in their age composed hymns to darkness, madness, destruction, which are all aspects of the struggle to live against death in life.

Even the technique of Jeffers's verse is hard like sharp, flying chips of a "streaming-shouldered tide rock," which dart into space, piercing the sleeping pools of our sensibilities and stirring their silences like the battle-cry of one drunk with light. Sometimes his poetry reads as though sentences had been left out; the reader must think between words. Being above all an imaginative artist, he invents a new form of expression. Jeffers's verse is

> Multitude, multitudes of thoughts,
> All fierce, all flesh-eaters musically clamorous;
> Bright hawks that hover and dart headlong.

Jeffers has a close form-relationship with the late, and now sadly neglected Irish poet, Philip Francis Little:

his almost perfect blank verse at times runs into un-
expected alexandrine:—

> I found myself emerging in midair
> a negligible quantity among
> huge integers, tremendous, primitive,
> deep sky, dark sea, bare plateau—nothing more,
> pervaded by a hush primordial,
> coeval with creation's seventh day.

and this from a longer, tragic poem where the silence
of death and the silence of nature:—

> appearing to possess affinity
> with skies above and with the sea that rolled
> blue billow round that mountain pedestal,
> upon the top of which Fate's sculptor hand
> had set so still an image—

Often one discovers such vividly and intensely felt
landscapes as:—

> Scarcely audible
> the rumoured sea-din here: so shakes the air
> when from her rocky den the lioness,
> aroused by famine, uttering sullenly
> her subdued roar, remote, on velvet paw,
> moves moaning through the troubled wilderness.

Poets like Little and Jeffers have what Coleridge regarded as "the power of acting creatively under laws
of its own origination."

Little is nearer than Jeffers to so called "pure poetry",

if for pure poetry we are willing to take Santayana's definition: "Pure Poetry is pure experiment."

Again we quote Santayana to make this clear:—"A poet is inspired because what occurs in his brain is a true experiment in creation."

Herbert Read in his *Form in Modern Poetry* speaks of "organic form." This organic form is considered as having its own inherent law, originating with its very invention and fusing in one vital unity structure and content. This more than any other analysis of modern poetical form seems to apply to Jeffers, the poet, or to any artist who works intuitively and not through imitative imagination. Elizabeth Drew in her admirable book, *Discovering Poetry,* explains why many of our modern poets intentionally exclude the logical or reasonable elements of thought from their poetry: "They deliberately organize poetic thought as a type of thought distinct in itself from all other types of thought." This statement is in accord with the theory of Read quoted above, and also with Benedetto Croce's opinion that every work of art is an independent organism in itself, and must be judged by its own laws. A. E. records the birth of poetry as follows: "How can we explain the mystery of the imagination, the power we discover in ourselves which leaps upon us, becoming master of ideas, images and words, taking control of these from the reasoning mind, giving to them symbolic meanings, until images, ideas and

words, swept together, become an intellectual organism
by some transcendental power superior to all reasoning?"

One particular attitude of mind is essential to an
understanding of Jeffers's poetry—the pagan. By pagan
we do not mean the narcissistic nostalgia of the nudist
cults now in vogue, nor Isadora Duncan with her
"idealistically conceived reproductive projects." By pagan we mean the traditional, distinctive classic paganism such as Wordsworth accepted:—

> I'd rather be
> A pagan suckled in a creed outworn.

The traditional paganism we have in mind has left
a definite, cultural perception in the modern man's
vision of the world without as well as of the life within.

In his dealings with truth or reality Jeffers recreates
the Aristotelean νοῦς ποιητικός through what we might
call the premeditative pagan thought; thought as the
combination of instinct, intuition and intelligence in
the outstanding minds of the ages. Jeffers surveys this
paganism as:—

> one power (the Greek δαίμων) you may call it
> God to the vulgar,
> Exists from eternity into eternity, all the
> protean phenomena, all forms, all faces of things,
> And all the negligible lightnings of consciousness
> Are made of that power.

Chesterton, sneered at by the mechanically inclined concrete realists, in his adroit, paradoxical apology for paganism comments as follows:—

"They (the pagans) were not satisfied with realism, because they never quite lost the sense of something more real than realism.

"Men like Shelley and Heine might get rid of religion, but they would not get rid of this great glamor of natural things, which seemed to make them preternatural."

Jeffers's poems may be moral or unmoral—but they are never immoral. Only a morbid mind could find uncleanness there. Opening any one of Jeffers's volumes, we find all the reasonable, respectable emotions of a Christian humanity emerging from it in a new and shameless paganism to startle and beguile with passionate, sympathetic directness. One of Jeffers's critics comments upon his superabundant and propitious force, but feels in him a lack of faith. How can anyone, even when only superficially acquainted with his poetry, accuse Jeffers of a lack of faith? "The universal God's beauty is better, I think, than to lip eagerly the mother's breast," he writes. Creeds have become to Jeffers "the trap that catches noblest spirits, that caught, they say, God when he walked on earth." Real faith, attained not spatially but spiritually, by the cosmic poet who has found spontaneous expression in his work—this faith is

no passion—but peace,
The pure flame and the white, fierier than any
passion; no time but spheral eternity.

Such faith is a kind of "intellectual auscultation," as
Bergson names it. So Jeffers leaves behind him the outworn orthodoxy of our forefathers, and

Lying on the hillside
Sick with those visions, I remembered
The knife in the stalk of my humanity;
I drew and it broke;
I entered the life of the grown forest
And the great life of the ancient peaks
The patience of stone,
I felt the changes in the veins
In the throat of the mountain,
A grain in many centuries.
We have our own time.

We see that Jeffers has hunted his God "like an eagle
upon the mountains," and has "killed monsters in the
chase." In *Truce and the Peace* he writes:

The robbers triumphed, the roof burned overhead;
The eternal living and untroubled god
Lying asleep upon a lily bed . . .
Men screamed, the bugle screamed, walls broke in the air,
We never knew till then that he was there.

Lines such as these could not have been written by
one lacking faith. We think of St. Augustine's, of Shelley's, of Wordsworth's, of Goethe's faith in connection
with Jeffers's. Faith based on the belief that mankind

can best be served and saved through cultivation and salvation of the individual.

In the true introvert, the *animus,* or surface-self, with its extraverted, rational knowledge, is submerged by the *anima*, or deeper self, through mystical or poetic knowledge of the Prime Mover. Not to feel or to be moved by this faith is to miss the fundamental meaning of Jeffers, the poet, when he emphasizes belief in the unity of life and in the soul that breathes through that universal unity, which he calls "the rhythm of that wheel. . . . Who can behold it is happy and will praise it to the people."

We must make ourselves equal to God; only thus can we apprehend him and his universe. Man, animals and plants do not die, but undergo a dissolution which is a renewal of organic life force. There may be an end of consciousness, but there is no beginning nor end of life. This is Jeffers's faith in the older concepts of humanity, which is "slavish in the mass; but at stricken moments it can shine terribly against the dark magnificence of things." Revolutions are deaths and resurrections.

The keynote of Jeffers's philosophy of life is in the four words "breaking out of humanity." To understand this phrase we must enter Jeffers's consciousness, observe that inner impetus of the poetic mind. Before doing this let us look into Nietzsche's *Zarathustra:*

O my brethren, am I then cruel? But I say: What
falleth, that shall one also push. Everything of today
—it falleth, it decayeth; who would preserve it. But
I, I wish also to push it. Break up, break up, I pray
you, the good and the just! O my brethren, have you
understood also this word?

Here Nietzsche teaches that nothing is stable, not
even values, not even the concepts of good and evil.
We cannot change social conditions in one lifetime.
To become endurable to ourselves an inner transformation is necessary before the individual can attach himself at least outwardly to the economic, intellectual and
political reality of his times. "Between acquisition and
conservation a dynamic equilibrium must continually
be established; but meanwhile an ever more active
critical spirit is attacking one tendency or the other,
examining without pity the ideas which are favored or
which hold the field, testing and discussing without
pity the tendencies of the adjustment which is always
obtained." Thus Paul Valery interprets what Nietzsche
calls to be cruel to oneself. Before accepting democracy, Nazism, communism, or what not, the thought-
ful individual should stop and ask himself, "How
nearly have we approached the solution of world problems since Heraclitus puzzled the Sophists? How
valuable is the vast so-called progress of the passing
twentieth century? What prospect does it open up to
us for the future?" Spengler in *Decline of the West*,
Proust in *A la Recherche du Temps Perdu,* and Jef-

fers's poems combine the answer to this collective world question.

Progress, rightly understood, is an outward expression of the inner growth of nations as well as of individuals. Let us consider the signs of progress as they exist in the world today. The present international financial crisis, or depression, is a sign of a downward movement in our civilization, derived originally from a war condition. We see that life has been robbed of its legitimate perspective and reduced to a material basis where too often the individual passions and impulses of political and economic tyrants hold sway, thus beclouding the thoughts of millions with fear, jealousy, discontent, and unrest. The door leading inward is left open for disappointment and "failure of nerve" to enter and take possession.

This "failure of nerve" is realistically revealed in Proust's monumental work, *A la Recherche du Temps Perdu*. Here is a vast panorama of the social and spiritual débâcle, a revelation of all the foibles of human society, of the perversities of the animal man, and of the relative insignificance of mathematical time. What is Charlus but the tragic symbol of a great civilization afflicted with an incurable malady—over-civilization? Most of the lives in Proust's novel are failures, his characters puppets of the eternal flux carrying with it not only people but places, social and political systems and customs, and constantly renewing the aspects and relationships of things. We cannot escape the tragic

synthesis forced upon us—that the degeneration of a
Charlus is the degeneration of an epoch in our history. "If, at least, there were granted me time enough
to complete my work, I would not fail to stamp it
with the seal of that Time the understanding of which
was this day so forcibly impressing itself upon me,
and I would therein describe men—even should that
give them the semblance of monstrous creatures—as
occupying in Time a place far more considerable than
the so restricted one allotted to them in space"—here
is the key to Proust.

Another indication of our deterioration is the casual-
ness with which we drift toward downfall, a condition
which Spengler characterizes as the prime phenomenon
of all past and future world history, the Faustian vision, and the Apollonian soul in an ever childish humanity:

> Every culture stands in a deeply symbolical, almost
> in a mystical relation to the Extended . . . the inward
> and the outward fulfilment, the finality, that awaits
> every living culture—is the purport of all the historic
> "declines," among them the decline of the classical
> we know so well and fully, and another decline en-
> tirely comparable to it in course and duration, which
> will occupy the first centuries of the coming millen-
> nium, but is heralded already and sensible in and
> around us to-day—the decline of the West.

If art be life objectified, if the true function of the
poet be to translate the vital into the verbal, the pres-

ent into the future, then surely Robinson Jeffers must be held the most significant poet of America since Walt Whitman. His vision of our toppling civilization has apocalyptic power.

Bergson has defined life as a struggle against matter; a constant tendency toward distribution of vital energy toward the world of the spirit. Marxism, that near-substitute for religion, is accepted by the extreme communist minority as an ethical as well as political organ for Bergson's vital energy. Nietzsche has called this vital energy in life "that which ever seeks beyond itself." This is perhaps as good a characterization as any of the creative poetic power shown in Jeffers's work. It is a power that repeats itself seemingly in the difficult periods of history, the times of the purification of humanity:

> Our people are clever and masterful;
> They have power in the mass, they accomplish
>   marvels.
> It is possible time will make them before it annuls
>   them, but at present
> There is not one memorable person, there is not one
>   mind to stand with the trees,
> One life with the mountains.

This is the vision of Job, of Dante, of the author of *The City of Dreadful Night*. Jeffers, with St. Augustine, teaches that all which exists in the Now, during our own stay of short duration on this planet, will be lost with our passing into Eeternity, into the Nietzschean "ring of rings," the Heraclitan "cosmic order, the same for all beings, no god nor man made, but it always was and is and will be, ever-living fire, blazing up and dying down in measure."

Jeffers has recaptured it thus:

> Out of the mother, and through the spring exultances,
>   ripeness and decadence; and home to the mother.
> You making haste on decay; not blameworthy; life is
>   good, be it stubbornly long or suddenly
> A mortal splendor.

We might justly call Jeffers our Sophocles, supreme in tragic tension; one who has introduced, or rather taken the first steps (among our modern American poets) in the fourth dimensional sphere with a progression that is of vital import to a new generation.

The tension of his feeling has been manifested from deeper traits of human nature than that of the so called great American poets of the past. His poetry gives us definite evidence of a dynamic release of the subconscious in a reality, or "universal forms more real than living man."

His poetic genius will not be completely recognized by his own generation; the giant of spiritual agony is helpless when surrounded by a majority of men who do not possess enough spirituality to raise them above the mere scientific and technical realities of the moment.

"Panem et circenses" still cry our mobs of flesh and bone, and *"regnum meum non est de hoc mundo"* reply the giants of spiritual agony to our jesting Pilates in the politico-capitalistic arena of today.

II. *HIS PHILOSOPHY*

Poetry is a more philosophical and a higher
thing than history; for poetry tends to express the universal, history the particular.
                                        Aristotle

HIS PHILOSOPHY

BY the universal is meant what we call nature, or what is supplied to the poet's conception by the forces outside himself. It is the liberty of genius to break through conventions, to create and justify new universal laws. It is the poet's right and duty to express as best he may his own essential philosophy, his "suspended judgment," as Montaigne calls it. In doing so he may lose himself to the world at large during his lifetime, as did Dante and Whitman in their generation. Perhaps that is because the poetic Icarian heights are so lofty and his sensibilities are so sharpened that the poet himself seldom understands his own motives; they are concealed in the plausible consciousness, since poets work intuitively, usually knowing nothing of pure reason. If the poets were too conscious of a philosophic system, they would cease to be poets. Yet, in saying this we do not mean to suggest an "antithesis between truth and poetry; they belong together" as Jeffers himself believes.

Like a bright hair of fire shining from Jeffers's second published volume, *Californians,* to his latest, we find this refrain—"breaking out of humanity." In this one phrase, as was shown in our first chapter, is concealed the poet's entire philosophy of life. No wonder the *Boston Transcript,* in reviewing his first important book, *Roan Stallion,* declared: "At present he is rather a curious pedant who often writes meaningless phrases, but who writes them with difference." It is this "difference" in writing, which at times takes the form of antithetical prose, that the poetic force becomes daemonic with the utterances of this poet who is both personal and individual. This new manner used by Jeffers in expressing his imaginative intent puzzled the readers of *Roan Stallion.* Jeffers's poetic conceptions are typical of prophets imbued with a mastering sense of their mission. The force of his creative imagination disrupts the reader like an electric drill boring into a rock; all is chaos and disorder in reading Jeffers for the first time. It is only when the current of the too powerful tension is switched off that one gets the proper perspective of the poet's vision. He is prophetic; he sees beyond the bounds of humanity into the future. Besides, the poet Jeffers is a man in whom creature and creator are united. "There is not only matter, excess, clay, mire, folly, chaos; but there is also the creator, the sculptor, the hardness of the hammer, the divinity of the spectator, and the seventh day."

Let us hear what Jeffers himself has to say about the meaning of "breaking out of humanity." "We have learned within the past century or so that humanity is only a temporary and infinitesimal phenomenon in a large universe. The knowledge involves a readjustment of values that can only be managed by looking at humanity objectively—from the outside. It seems to me wasteful that almost the whole of human energy is expended inward, on itself, in loving, hating, governing, cajoling, amusing, its own members. It is like a new-born babe, conscious almost exclusively of its own processes and whence its food comes from. As the child grows up, its attention must be drawn from itself to the more important world outside it. In a civilization like ours—metropolitanism intensified by machinery—human nature (which we developed under very different conditions) becomes an anachronism. We can't turn back the civilization, not at least until it collapses, and our descendants will have to develop a new sort of nature—will have to 'break out of humanity' or suffer considerably—probably both."

We, the children of this century, have made a great din, the noise of many lost battles, the whir of many machines on land, sea and air, to hide a "silence within" ourselves. In this tyranny of scientific materialism and of political enslavement, work has become drudgery. When the will of humanity is thwarted and weakened through a pernicious social system, man becomes unhealthy and willing to destroy if only for the sake of destruction, then gradually reverts to a primitive state (the new-born babe's state). This is true of American civilization today.

The result is downfall. As Spengler analyzes the

situation, we are entering the last phase of decline. The huge Colossus which man has so carefully reared is crushing him.

As Professor Whitehead holds, life now more than ever has become "an offensive against the repetitive mechanism of the universe."

We have bartered culture for mechanization and in Spengler's words we are "spiritually dead men" living in the "autumnal cities" of past cultures.

The poet, E. Merrill Root, has directly felt and expressed this spiritually dead state in a poem *Down Among the Dead Men:*

> This would not be such a frustrate world
> If the dead would only die;
> When, oh when, shall we shovel them in
> To be the grasses' origin?
> When shall death end and life begin
> For live men under the sky?

A character in Celene's *Journey to the End of the Night* says: "there are just ordinary madmen and there are madmen who're in agony over the set form of civilization."

It does seem that a new, tragic defence has been developed in the creative mind of Jeffers, Root, Spender, Roy Campbell and others whose mental outlook on life in general corresponds to the philosophy of Whitehead.

Civilization is shackled by a system of monstrous

organization. "Never before in history has the micro-
cosm so displayed its superiority to the macrocosm.
The Faustian soul is enslaved to a new matter, emerging out of its early beginnings in the simple machine."
With the losing of religion, or what Lenin called "the
opium of the people," "materialism has made a special
appeal to those who have been used to an authorita-
tive religion and now have lost their faith in it," as
Bertrand Russell puts it. At present the creative energy
of man works out in the study of natural science, sociology, politics and economic welfare. The practical
leaders of today—Edison, Marconi, Marx and Einstein
—have replaced the more theoretical Kant, Darwin and
Huxley. As long as the task of the scientist is incom-
plete, so long will the poet and the philosopher soar
above the tyrannic finalities of science, they, the
scientists, "having no function but to serve and support
civilization, the enemy of man," according to Jeffers.

When we have solved to a temporary satisfaction
the political, social and economic problems now weigh-
ing so heavily upon our over-mechanized world, we
shall still be tormented more than ever by that human
problem, the problem of the individual, the problem
of death and the immortality of the soul. D. H. Lawrence has said: "The individual alone can save humanity alive. But the greatest of great individuals must
have deep, throbbing roots down in the dark red soil
of the living flesh of humanity."

To a certain type of the ultra-modern, pseudoscientific mind, this idea of "breaking away from humanity" must seem fantastic. As Jeffers says these are

> not of the sad race of Prometheus,
> to waste "themselves" in Favor of the future.

They are lovers of·

> a blond favorite,
> A Father of lights and noises, wars, weeping and
>   laughter,
> Hot labor, lust and delight and the other blemishes.

But if the soul of the average thinking individual has a reason for existence, it seems to Jeffers, it must sooner or later, if only momentarily, emerge and enter into this state of "breaking away." This attitude might be classified as psychotic, anti-social, anti-institutional.

The typically Jeffersean philosophy is to be found in the poem, *Meditation on Saviors.* Here the poet gives us the inward and outward vision of his whole endeavor—the keynote to the human attitude embodied in his philosophy. In Part I, stanzas 3 and 4, we see Jeffers's cosmic theory of breaking away from the individual self into the vital not-self—the Nirvana motif. We find here also the poet's indifference to politics and political systems, be they capitalistic or Marxian. Theoreticians of the proletariat will find in Jeffers no "passive suffering of the masses or their slavish submissiveness" to capitalism. Nor will they find in his poetry the art of the dominant classes. Jeffers has no interest in a particular class to which he gives his allegiance;

hence his poetry is not an art-tool for any definite worldly propaganda. Perhaps Jeffers's poetry is the poetry of an age in which feelings and thoughts cannot find incarnation. He has the inwardness, the self-knowledge, the Socratic *sophrosyne,* an ability to live above this civilization, which puts all materialistic theories and all little worldly advantage-seekers to shame:

> Here on the rock it is great and beautiful, here on the
> foam-wet granite sea-fang it is easy to praise
> Life and water and the shining stones; but whose cat-
> tle are the herds of the people that one should
> love them?
>
> If they were yours, then you might take a cattle-
> breeder's delight in the herds of the future. Not
> yours.
> Where the power ends let love, before it sours to
> jealousy. Leave the joys of government to Caesar.

In the following stanzas Jeffers meditates on the saviors of humanity, among them Christ. Knowing that a Caesar cannot save the world and that his power always ends in the "blood-hate," the poet writes:—

> The apes of Christ lift up their hands to praise love:
> but wisdom without love is the present savior,
> Power without hatred, mind like a many-bladed ma-
> chine subduing the world with deep indifference.
>
> The apes of Christ itch for a sickness they have never
> known; words and the little envies will hardly

Measure against that blinding fire behind the tragic
eyes (of Christ) they have never dared to con-
front.

In the second part of the poem Jeffers tells how he
found among the hills at Point Lobos, once purified by
a great conflagration, his own creative power and deep
poetic vision from contemplation of nature's tragedies, those of the Greeks, and the life of Christ:

As for the people,
I have found my rock, let them find theirs.

Let them lie down at Caesar's feet and be saved; and
he in his time reap their daggers and gratitude.

In Part III the human Jeffers reveals himself:

Yet I am the one made pledges against the refuge con-
tempt, that easily locks the world out of doors.
This people as much as the sea-granite is part of the
God from whom I desire not to be fugitive.

In the fourth part of the poem, Jeffers the deter-
minist, or what modern psychology terms associationist,
appears. The Greeks called determinism Fate, believing that the entire complex organism of man is bound-
ed by his natural inheritance. Jeffers's work shows the
influence of three types of determinism: The Grecian
Fate familiar to him through his comprehensive ac-
quaintance with the classics, that of his Presbyterian
inheritance and up-bringing with its doctrine of pre-
destination, and the grip upon his mind exerted by

the theory of scientific determinism unescapable by one who has devoted years to the study of science, including medical biology and bacteriology.

> How should one caught in the stone of his own person
>   dare to tell the people anything but relative to
>   that?
> But if a man could hold in his mind all the conditions
>   at once, of man and woman, of civilized
>
> And barbarous, of sick and well, of happy and under
>   torture, of living and dead, of human and not
> Human, and dimly all the human future—what
>   should persuade him to speak? and what could
>   his words change?

Again in the third stanza which might be called the high song of determinism:

> The mountain ahead of the world is not forming but
>   fixed. But the man's words would be fixed also,
> Part of that mountain, under equal compulsion; under
>   the same present compulsion in the iron con-
>   sistency.
>
> And nobody sees good or evil but out of a brain a
>   hundred centuries quieted, some desert
> Prophet's, a man humped like a camel, gone mad be-
>   tween the mud-walled village and the mountain
>   sepulchres.

There is a close similitude between Jeffers's determined pessimism and that of Hardy's "cruel Nature's law." "The scheme of things is indeed incomprehensible" wrote Hardy to an English poet "and there I suppose we must leave it, perhaps for the best. Knowledge might be terrible."

In one of his last poems Hardy expresses the same idea:

> O My soul, keep the rest unknown!
> It is too like a sound of moan
> When the charnel-eyed
> Pale Horse has nighed:
> Yea, none shall gather what I hide!

With Part IV we come to a very important aspect of Jeffers's philosophy and use of symbolism, namely, blood-sacrifice. This ancient rite is frequently referred to by Tacitus, Plutarch, Suetonius, and Ceasar in his writings about the Celts. Jeffers scores America by accusing her of having not outgrown blood-sacrifice:

> *This* people has not outgrown blood-sacrifice, one
>   must writhe on the high cross to catch at their
>   memories;
> The price is known. I have quieted love: for love of
>   the people I would not do it (engage in war).
>   For power (spiritual) I would do it.
>
> But that stands against reason: what is power to a
>   dead man, dead under torture?—What is power
>   to a man
> Living, after the flesh is content? Reason is never a
>   root, neither of act or desire.

> For power living (worldly power) I would never do
> it; they are not delightful to touch, one wants to
> be separate. For power
> After the nerves are put away underground, to lighten
> the abstract unborn children toward peace . . .

But, in spite of his declared attitude, Jeffers's concern for humanity will not let him rest:

> Yet look: are they not pitiable? No: if they lived
> forever they would be pitiable.
> But a huge gift reserved quite overwhelms them at
> the end (death); they are able then to be still
> and not cry.

They have "touched a little of the beauty, and seen a little of the beauty of things . . ."

> They are not to be pitied but very fortunate; they
> need no savior, salvation (death) comes and takes
> them by force.
> It gathers them into the great kingdom of dust and
> stone, the blown storms, the stream's-end ocean.

In the above Jeffers touches upon the atomistic Lucretian conception of immortality.

The two last stanzas are typical electrifying utterances of Jeffers's poetic intensity reaching a height of pure mysticism:

> But while he lives let each man make his health in his
> mind, to love the coast opposite humanity
> And so be freed of love, laying it like bread on the
> waters; it is worst turned inward, it is best shot
> farthest.

Love, the mad wine of good and evil, the saint's and
    murderer's, the mote in the eye that makes its
    object
Shine the sun black; the trap in which it is better to
    catch the inhuman God than the hunter's own
    image.

III. MYSTICISM AND SYMBOLISM

Now I a fourfold vision see,
And a fourfold vision is given to me;
'Tis not a fourfold in my supreme delight
And threefold in soft Beulah's night
And twofold Always. May God us keep
From Single vision and Newton's sleep.
Blake

MYSTICISM AND SYMBOLISM

WE must bear in mind that from Plotinus to A. E. the mystical vision, or "will as vision," is to be considered as an individual psychological experience and therefore judged on personal grounds. What T. S. Eliot says of poetry might be applied also to mysticism: "Criticism of course never does find out what poetry is in the sense of arriving at an adequate definition, nor can criticism ever arrive at any final appraisal of poetry."

The direct subconscious power revealed and liberated in the mystic's psyche is a contact with a reality beyond definitions. We all feel that the mystic vision is something far beyond small, literal, inert egotistical wishes which make man only "a bridge to the superman." To Blake, "self-annihilation" was the source of "veritable inspiration." To Yeats "wisdom speaks in poetic images." A. E. admits that he utters many things of which he himself is unaware.

Truly Ouspensky says: "This explains why a man who has had mystical experiences uses, for expressing and transmitting them, those forms of images, words and speech which are best known to him, which he is accustomed to use most often, and which are the most typical and characteristic for him. In this way it may

47

easily happen that different people describe and convey
an entirely identical experience quite differently." In
relation to the idea of hidden (personal) knowledge,
mysticism may be regarded as a breaking through of
hidden consciousness, or, as Jeffers expresses it:

> seeking to give myself I sought
> Outward in vain through all things, out through God,
> And tried all heights, all gulfs, all dreams, all thought.
> I found this wisdom on the wonderful road, the es-
> sential me cannot be given away,
> The single Eye, God cased in blood-shaped clay.

This essential I and Me, the hidden knowledge of
the mystic poet's psyche, cannot be given away to
reason. In inspired moments the mystic, to quote Jeffers once more, sees

> his own mind
> Objectively, all the current sand courses at one mo-
> ment.

and "the soul crescents or wanes between the nights
of centuries," and

> voices
> Tell you like singing fires and you looked up at mid-
> night and saw wings astonishing the darkness.

A similar power is achieved by Brontë in *Wuthering
Heights;* by her the ultimate, tragi-mystical suspense
is conveyed through a larger apprehension than by the
enigmatic Emily Dickinson or by Elinor Wylie.

In a poetic fragment, *The Prisoner,* Emily Brontë
reveals in a moment's vision as overwhelmingly as Jeffers the vicissitudes of a mystic mind:—

> Oh!—dreadful is the check—intense the agony—
> When the ear begins to hear, and the eye begins to see,
> When the pulse begins to throb, the brain to think again;
> The soul to feel the flesh, and the flesh to feel the chain.
> Yet I would loose no sting, would wish no torture less;
> The more that anguish racks, the earlier it will bless;
> And robed in fires of hell, or bright with heavenly shine,
> If it but herald death, the vision is divine!

Blake's power of mystic vision is best expressed in
his own words:

> In Great Eternity every particular form gives forth or
>   Emanates
> Its own peculiar Light, and the form is the Divine
>   Vision
> And the Light is his Garment. This is Jerusalem in
>   every Man,
> A Tent and Tabernacle of Mutual Forgiveness, Male
>   and Female clothings.
> And Jerusalem is called Liberty.

This spontaneous activity of the mystic poet's psyche,
so Jung informs us, "often becomes so intense that visionary pictures are seen or inner voices heard. These
are manifestations of the spirit directly experienced today as they have been from time immemorial."

Jeffers's is not the beatific but the apocalyptic vision
—"as if it were a mountain burning with fire cast into

the sea." He belongs to the philosophic-minded mystics. The conception that dominates his poems is that of a supreme, all-pervading Power in which all things are one, a being somewhat like the Grecian Pan, that all-healing god of the Universe. He sees the cosmic system unfolding itself, step by step, from unity to multiplicity, and returning to unity again. His ideas are often difficult to unravel, and his appeal is to mystical intuition rather than to pure reason.

A. Brockington in his profound study *Mysticism and Poetry* writes: "There is a mystical element of poetry, though the poet, as such, is not a mystic, in the traditional sense. In that sense he is, as Bremond calls him, a *mystique manqué*. The true poet however, has always the mystical outlook; and so has everyone who recognizes the poetry of existence."

Jeffers's mysticism goes back to Sufism, the belief of the Mohammedan mystics who have purified themselves from all worldly defilement. Jeffers has found Nirvana on earth; flesh no longer strives with spirit; reunion with universal intelligence has taken place; all past acts have been nullified; there is absolute detachment—a "blown-out candle" state, a realized identity with the Absolute, and the peace which comes with it—a state in which we perceive "the calm and proud procession of eternal things."

Consistency is not to be found in mystics. They believe in a transcendant cause in the world, an imper-

sonal and unmoral God, mysteriously identical with
ourselves.

Says Shelley:—

> The awful shadow of some unseen power
> Floats though unseen among us,—visiting
> This various world with as inconstant wing
> As summer winds . . .

"If any teach Nirvana is to cease, say unto such they
lie. If any teach Nirvana is to live, say unto such they
err." Thus spoke a Buddhist in the seventh century.
In short, Nirvana is the urge to alienate ourselves from
ourselves in order to transcend ourselves and become
timeless.

D. H. Lawrence, who arrived at the Palace of the
Absolute by way of the long road of excess, knew too
well this anagogical state: "There are myriads of human lives that are not absolute nor timeless; myriads
that just waver and toss temporarily, never become
more than relative, never come into being. They have
no being, no immortality." In the Cabbala we read that
"there is no work of the Holy One but from darkness,
and there is no good but from evil." In other words,
suffering is a means through which the Absolute or
Timeless may be attained. The key-words to Budd-
hism are "enlightenment through suffering": to the
Christian the key-words are "love through endurance." Thus, through these two extremes, Jeffers has

found the ways of God and realized that:—

> Humanity is needless—
> Humanity is the start of the race, the gate to break
>   away from, the coal to kindle,
> The blind mask crying to be slit with eyeholes.

To the mystic the world becomes outworn, a troubling limbo. Thus man, shut away from his brothers who dwell in the Land of Vision, is, according to Blake, "a darkened being not yet called Albion"— man. To Jeffers humanity is still in the stage of animal consciousness, where self has become a disease, where "the desire of acquiring and grasping objects, or of enslaving men and animals, in order to minister to the self, becomes one of the main motives of life; and when, owing to this deep, fundamental division of human nature and consciousness, minds are tormented with a sense of sin, and their bodies with a myriad forms of disease." Jeffers has undoubtedly reached a state of consciousness where mere knowledge "loses its tentative, illusive form of thought, and acquires a cosmic, universal character." It becomes luminous with far-reaching interpretations, and

> the speckled tissue of universe
> Drew into one formed and rounded light.

Jeffers's mysticism belongs to that called by Buddha (according to the Pali canon) *Tathāgata* (he who has come to Reality) through meditation within *"samsāra"*, or the circle of births and deaths.

In the following lines Jeffers gives us his own résumé of mysticism:—

> He (Buddha) believes that nothing is real except as
>   we make it.
> I humbler have found in my blood
> Bred west of Caucasus a harder mysticism.
> Multitude stands in my mind but I think that the
>   ocean in the bone vault is only
> The bone vault's ocean; out there is the ocean's:
> The water is the water, the cliff is the rock, come
>   shocks and flashes of reality. The mind
> Passes, the eye closes, the spirit is a passage;
> The beauty of things was born before eyes and suf-
>   ficient to itself: the heart-breaking beauty
> Will remain when there is no heart to break for it.

In his introduction to *The Symbolic Movement in Literature,* Arthur Symons defines symbolism as "an unseen reality apprehended by the consciousness . . . of the poet." Edmund Wilson calls symbolism "an attempt by carefully studied means, a complicated association of ideas represented by a medley of metaphors, to communicate unique personal feelings." Joseph Wood Krutch in *Experience and Art* writes: "We think and we understand, not with things, but with words, with symbols and with syllogisms." "In a symbol," says Carlyle, "there is a concealment and yet revelation." And this from a modern psychoanalyst's point of view: "Symbols dominate to an unbelievable extent man's conduct and behavior as well as his thinking; they are the bridge over which he travels from the known to the unknown; from the more primitive to the more complex."

All the above-mentioned definitions agree in assigning to symbolism a combination of concealment and revelation. We cannot approach nor understand Blake's "manifold vision" without familiarizing ourselves with his personal symbolism, which he himself speaks of as a "symbolic art, vivifying all things and all words through imaginative connection with the human form."

The poet's "myriad symbols

> Are the masks o' the Cosmos; and Man's jobs
> To mak' myriads mair, a new Imitation.
> Confrontin' the impassive eternal universe
> Wi' the states o' his restless heart?

writes Hugh M'Diarmid the representative poet of the modern Scottish Renaissance group.

As Jeffers moves symbolically among the remote beginnings of the world and poetically presents his vision to our generation, we must accept him as a voice in which there is an echo of something far beyond the present moment. He brings back the breath of past times, and renews the promise of a better humanity. One might say of him what Emerson said of himself during his time—that his fame was the measure of the limitations of his age. When this is taken into consideration, we can approach Jeffers and the twofold purpose in his use of symbolism.

John Huizinga explains symbolism from the causal point of view thus: "Symbolism appears as a sort of short circuit of thought. Instead of looking for the relation between two things by following the hidden detours of their causal connections, thought makes a leap and discovers their relation, not in connection of cause or effects, but in a connection of signification or finality. Embracing all nature and all history, symbolism gave a conception of the world, of a still more vigorous unity, than that which modern science can offer."

If we do not accept Prometheus as the symbol of Shelley's own mind, or as the embodiment of his *Lapis Philosophorum,* then there is very little left of that sempiternal beauty in his poetry which forces itself in such intensified effect upon the reader as the very "white radiance of eternity."

To all philosophic poets, symbols are reminders of that invisible substance of reality which, no matter how definite they may be in essence, can never be fully expressed to the physical eye. In most of his longer poems Jeffers deals with primitive people, people who believe in forces, influences and events which, though imperceptible to sense, are nevertheless real. Lévy-Bruhl in his book, *Primitive Mentality,* says: "The Reality in which primitives live is itself mystical. Not a single being or object or natural phenomenon in their collective representation is what it appears to be to our mind.

Almost everything that we perceive therein either escapes their attention or is a matter of indifference to them. On the other hand, they see many things there of which we are unconscious."

In almost all of his longer poems Jeffers has created types endowed with a "quiescent ancestral memory, vision, or secret life." This "memory" is aroused, according to psychologists, by some abnormal stimulus. In the words of Yeats: "There is for every man some one scene, some one adventure, some one picture, that is the image of his secret life; for wisdom first speaks in images." Conrad Aiken, the solicitous solipsist among our lyric poets, asks:—"What is a symbol?" and replies:—

> Catch a beam in your hands, a beam of light,
> One bright golden beam, fledgling of dust,
> Hold it a moment, and feel its heart, and feel
> Ethereal pulse of light between your fingers:
> Then let it escape from you, and find its home
> In darkness, mother of light: and this will be
> Symbol of symbol, clue to clue, auricle of heart.

Jeffers's favorite symbols are the stallion and the eagle, Aiken's the fabulous unicorn and the bird of paradise which never perches, because he wings "in the pure aether of a thought, unthinking of endings or beginnings."

Reading *Telestai, Senlin,* and Aiken's ripest *tour de force, Preludes for Memnon,* is to see Arthur Davies's paintings, hear Debussy's music and at the same time realize that introspection is Aiken's God always seeking "Mother Chaos" (the poetic mind).

In order to follow the adventure of the inner world's deep confirmation, one must live wholly in the eternal Now, where exist no longer the past nor the future, and where the present has no duration. These visionaries, these Stoic-Epicurean accepters of the world, strike us at times as being a hundred years old. Yet, as Marcus Aurelius said: "A man of forty, possessing the most moderate intelligence, may be said to have seen all that is past and that is to come."

Lévy-Bruhl characterizes the mental life of these ancestral memory types as "clear instances of what we shall call mystic abstraction which, different as it is from logical abstraction, is none the less the process which primitive mentality would frequently make use of." St. Francis is a striking example of this type of mentality. Of him Bonaventura writes: "At the mere mention of the love of the Lord, he was aroused, moved, and enkindled, as though the inner chords of his heart vibrated under the bow of the voice without."

In Jeffers's *Tower beyond Tragedy* it was Cassandra to whom the god, Apollo, gave

> For a bride-gift prophecy and I took it for a treasure,
> I, a fool, I a maiden . . .
> Eight years I have seen the phantoms
> Walk up and down this stair; and the rocks groan in
>   the night, the great stones move

When no man sees them . . .
I am not Cassandra
But a counter of sunrises, permitted to live because I
    am crying to die.

In *Tamar* Aunt Stella is a "voice of the world of the dead." An unforgettable picture is made of the scene in a rocky fjord by the sea where gather old Stella, the poor idiot, Jinny, and Tamar. A male voice, ostensibly that of some prehistoric Indian chief, speaks from Aunt Stella's throat, bidding the girl dance on the shore.

So Tamar weeping
Slipped every sheath down to her feet, the spirit of
    the place
Ruling her, she and the evening star sharing the
    darkness,
And danced on the naked shore
Where a pale couch of sand covered the rocks,
Danced with slow steps and streaming hair,
Dark and slender
Against the pallid sea-gleam, slender and maidenly
Dancing and weeping . . .
It seemed to her that all her body
Was touched and troubled with polluting presences
Invisible, and whatever had happened to her from her
    two lovers
She had been until that hour inviolately a virgin
Whom now the desires of dead men and dead gods
    and dead tribes
Used for their common prey . . . dancing and
    weeping,
Slender and maidenly . . .

In *The Coast Range Christ* the great vision of David
Carrow, "a youth with wide and simple eyes", was

> "Love, love, we are mixed in the fire, the fire of the
>   world
> Ending, heavens beginning, spirits set free, the seas
>   burned, the stars hurled,
> All the promises have come true, I love you, I love
>   you, Lord."

In *The Women at Point Sur* Onorio Vasquez "with
his eyes like desert caves dreamed atonement," and
kept himself "virgin for the sake of his visions."

> Onorio Vasquez
> Never sees anything to the point. What he sees:
> The ocean like sleek gray stone perfectly joined
> To the heads and bays, a woman walking upon it,
> The curling scud of the storm around her ankles,
> Naked and strong, her thighs the height of the moun-
>   tain, walking and weeping,
> The heavy face hidden in the hands, the lips drinking
>   the tears in the hollow hands and the hair
> Streaming north. "Why are you so sad, our lady?"
> "I had only one son."

This vision was the outcome of Onorio's watching a
hawk being crucified on a barn wall.

In *The Loving Shepherdess* we again meet Onorio
with

> wealth
> Of visions, but those are not coinable. A power in
>   his mind

Was more than equal to the life he was born to,
But fear, or narrowing future, had kept it shut
From a larger life; the power wasted itself
In making purposeless visions, himself perceived them
To have no meaning relative to any known thing: but
    always
They made him different from his brothers: they gave
    him
A kind of freedom; they were the jewels and value of
    his life.

Mark Reave in *Thurso's Landing*:

                                following his vision
With no mind for this world, questioned it hard
About that other, he ate its fallacious answers
Together with his own doubts, like a starved man
    gulping
The meal with the weevils. "Life's all dream," it said,
"And death is a better, more vivid immortal dream,
But love is real; both are made out of love
That's never perfect in life, and the voids in it
Are the pains of life; but when our ungainly loads
Of blood and bone are thrown down, then the voids
    close,
Love becomes perfect, all's favor and immediate joy
For then we are what we love."

To summarize the psychology of these visionaries of Jeffers we might quote a phrase from Goethe: "The more particular represents the more general, not as a dream or shade, but as a vivid, instantaneous revelation of the inscrutable."

For his symbols as well as his philosophy, we must go back to Buddha and the Greeks in order to interpret Jeffers's poetry. What the leit-motif, or the association of musical themes with the dramatic ideas and personages or cross-currents of musical thoughts was to Richard Wagner, the use of poetic symbols is to Jeffers—the Teutonic Valhalla versus the Buddhistic Nirvana.

Behind the mystic world-drama of *Gotterdamme-rung* lies a very modern conception: the *Ring des Nibelungen* is a poetic embodiment of the ideas and philosophic speculations that were of deep interest to Wagner and his time. The philosophic ground-work of the dramas is Schopenhauer's pessimism and atheism; politically, they grip with the problem of capitalism versus communism. With the end of *Gotterdammerung* ends the race of the Volsungs, created by Wotan to save the world from the power of the self-seeking Nibelungs.

A modern use of symbolism on a grand scale is Thomas Mann's present-day *Pilgrim's Progress* of introgression, *The Magic Mountain*. In a chapter called "Snow" Mann introduces, among other introspective workings of the human mind during a period of instability and unrest, the realization of the meaning of "expiation by blood," or what Jeffers calls "blood sacrifice." Empirical realities and metaphysical truths, earthly Hell and earthly Paradise, meet on this symbolic mountain. Symbolic it is meant to be, for Mann in his informal foreword says: "Our story has of its own nature something of the legend about it now and again." Among the blissful and tragic experiences on this mountain with its veil-like, Maya atmosphere, suffered by Hans Castorp at the time of his vision, is his making of "a dream poem of humanity" to which he will cling. He has learned from "those up there" of man's state, of his courteous and enlightened social state, behind which is always the temple in which the horrible blood-sacrifice is consummated. Although "from love and sweetness alone can form come— friendly, enlightened, beautiful human intercourse," it is "always in silent recognition of the blood sacrifice." We must remember that the novel itself ends—or is broken—by the world war—blood sacrifice.

A Vedic proverb says: "Sacrifice is the navel of the world." Blood sacrifice as regeneration, rebirth, the *causa prima* welded with the *finis ultimus,* is symbolized by the Greeks in the stories of Prometheus and of Iphigenia

> blameless white maid
> Whose delicate soft throat the thing that cuts sheep
> open was drawn across by a priest's hand.

Blood sacrifice is seen breaking out, not only before the Christian era but also after it, through superstition, intolerance, race prejudice, political and economic war, and revolution. It is as vehement a passion of the hu-

man psyche as religion, in which it had its origin as an
ancient rite. "The child at birth is the symbol of humanity making its way to life through a pathway of
blood," says Havelock Ellis in his post-war essays. If
humanity obeys "government which bases its power
on murder . . . if murder through war is to be al-
lowed," to quote Tolstoi, then the death knell of blood-
sacrifice will never be sounded. The average man still
believes, with the late Theodore Roosevelt, that "America, if she is to play a part in this world, must per-
form those sanguinary deeds of heroism which have
brought glory to a nation in the past, for only in war
can a nation acquire energy which is necessary in the
struggle of existence."

Walter Rathenau, himself a victim of "blood-sacrifice", came to this conclusion: "No one can redeem
himself, but every one can redeem another, class for
class, man for man; thus is a people redeemed."

Jeffers understands blood-sacrifice in the sense of
what Solomon Reinach calls "the fundamental errors
of humanity":

> War, torture, famine; oppression; the secret cruelties;
>   the plague in the air that killed its millions, that
>   child
> Reaping a fly's wings, innocently laughing
> From the rich heart? Oh it has no laughter though a
>   child. It is tortured with its own earnestness, it
>   is tortured. . . . . .

And

> Self-regardful humanity cutting itself away from the
> earth and the creatures, gathered home on itself,
> Digging a pit behind it and a gulf before it, cancer-
> ous, a growth that makes itself alien: How long
> would you be spared before the knife rings you
> and the spreading
> Ulcer scooped out, but this sound flesh solders you
> home to the beasts?
> O fortunate earth; you must find someone of the fu-
> ture, against the wolf in men's hearts.

Jeffers sees with Karl Marx that "no greater mis-
fortune can happen to a nation than to conquer another nation." Conscience revolts again the capitalistic
practice of war-suicide of peoples and civilizations.

In his *Liberation of America* Calverton calls Jeffers
"more than il-logical; he is a-logical in his whole approach to life." From the psychological and mystical
points of view Jeffers is not "a-logical" but pre-logical;
he draws his meanings from age-old symbols, never
from arguments.

J. C. Powys, our sceptical Epicurus defending the
illogical, writes: For the illogical is not necessarily the
unintelligible, so long as the reason which we use is that
same imaginative and clairvoyant reason, which, in its
higher measure, sustains the vision of the poets and the
artists.

In *The Women at Point Sur* Jeffers comments upon his own use of figures and symbols:

> I was quiet . . .
>
> Imagination, the traitor of the mind, has taken my
>   solitude and slain it.
> No peace but many companions: the hateful-eyed
> And human-bodied are all about me: you that love
>   multitude may have them.
>
> But why should I make fables again? There are many
> Tellers of tales to delight women and the people.
> I have no vocation. The old rock under the house, the
>   hills with their hard roots and the ocean hearted
> With sacred quietness from here to Asia
> Make me ashamed to speak of the active little bodies,
>   the coupling bodies, the misty brainfuls
> Of perplexed passion. Humanity is needless.
> I said, "Humanity is the start of the race, the gate to
>   break away from, the coal to kindle.
> The blind mask crying to be slit with eye-holes."
> Well, now it is done, the mask slit, the rag burnt, the
>   starting-post left behind; but not in a fable.
> Culture's outlived, art's root cut, discovery's
> The way to walk in. Only remains to invent the lan-
>   guage to tell it. Match-ends of burnt experience
> Human enough to be understood,
> Scraps and metaphors will serve. The wine was a
>   little too strong for the new wine-skins . . .

Here we are made to feel the longing of the super-man; man has become something that must be surpassed. Jeffers is pervaded with Oriental pessimism. The soul craves for rest, which it will never find so long as it is turning with the wheel; escape is possible only in Nirvana. Even Plato in *Critias* expresses this pessimism: "In times past the divine nature flourished in men; but at length, being mixed with mortal custom, it fell into ruin, hence an inundation of evils in the race." We feel through all this the cycle of involution which precedes the cycle of evolution. The wheel, the cosmic circle of life, is turning backward instead of forward. But descent to the dead is descent to eternally renewing nature. "Keep out and you shall keep in," said the all-wise Lao-tse, referring to the inhibited, repressed lives of human beings in a phrase worthy of Freud himself. Entering Jeffers's world, however, we do not abandon all hope as in Dante's infernal limbo. Jeffers's humanity—"the blind mask crying to be slit with eye-holes"—is a hopeful humanity. Being an imaginative poet, Jeffers invents a new way of using symbolism, for great imaginations can never rest content with familiar symbols. It is Jeffers's revaluation of world-old symbols, mistaken for a purely intellectual process, that puzzles the readers and critics.

Among his most frequently used symbols, or words conveying symbolic meanings, is "darkness." Darkness was the mystery of all mysteries to the Egyptians. The Psalms speak of God making darkness his secret place. Dante moves in darkness. Blake writes in his *Preludium to America:*

The shadowy daughter of Urthona stood before red
    Orc, when fourteen suns had journeyed o'er his
    dark abode;
Crowned with a helmet and dark hair the nameless
    female stood,
The newborn female America, born out of darkness.

But to Jeffers darkness is really light, dazzling and blinding, the womb of rebirth which is resurrection. In *Night* he writes:

Over the dark mountain, over the dark pinewood,
Down the long dark valley along the shrunken river,
Returns the splendor without rays, the shining of
    shadow,
Peace-bringer, the matrix of all shining and quieter
    of shining.

In *The Woman at Point Sur* he describes the Reverend Barclay:

Roofed with terrible centuries of silent darkness he
    stumbled, and the world
Dissolved in a moment. After a moment's error in the
    gulf of emptiness
He leaned and touched the hill with his hand, he
    modelled with his hand room enough to crouch
    on, and slowly,
Painfully, element by element, sun moved the world
    back,
Willed it to being, and with the pain of creation.

The symbolic word used next most frequently after "darkness" by Jeffers is "stone." It seems almost as though rocks symbolize for him the history of the human mind. To primitive man stones, like trees, symbolized strength, power, vitality, endurance—all the qualities prized by men in their early and later days. The Mithraic phrase, "God out of the rock", means the indwelling, higher self with its power of will to action, the *atma-buddhi*.

In the *Rigveda* we read. "I place this circle of stones for the living; it is a heap which can keep death at a distance." Fraser gives instances of a belief among the Bavarians that bodily suffering can be healed on the face of rocks. Grecian mothers used to strip their children when they were sick and push them into holes in rocks to cure them.

In a poem called *To the House* Jeffers speaks of stones as

> the bones of the old mother
> To build us a hold against the hosts of the air;
> Granite the blood-heat of her youth
> Held molten in hot darkness against the heart.

In another accompanying the above entitled *To the Rock That Will Be a Corner-stone of the House* he addresses the rock thus:

> Lend me the stone strength of the past and I will
>   lend you
> The wines of the future, for I have them.
> How dear you will be to me when I too grow old,
>   old comrade.

And in the next poem, *The Stone-cutter*:

> Yet stones have stood for a thousand years, and pained
>   thoughts found
> The honey peace in old poems.

A much used and, by his readers and critics, a much misunderstood symbol in Jeffers's poetry is "death." Not the mediaeval or eighteenth century romantic poets' Death; but death as the Greeks understood it in the Homeric "Ὕπνῳ καὶ Θανάτῳ διδυμάοσιν", Hesiod's "son of night," and Aeschylus's "everlasting endless sleep." Jeffers likens death to

> The swoon of fulfilment of love in some lovelier vale
>   among flowers is the languor that flushes us;
> O why did we fear him? For Death
> Is a beautiful youth and his eyes are sleepy, the lids
>   droop heavily with wine
> When he wakens.

Elsewhere he speaks of death as "a starved man dreaming bread". In *The Tower beyond Tragedy*:

> O grave and kindly
> Last of the words of earth, I pray you
> Lead my substance
> Speedily into another shape, make me grass,
> Death, make me stone,
> Make me air to wander free between the stars and the
>   peaks; but cut humanity
> Out of my being, that is the word that
> Festers in me,

Not captivity, not my enemies; you will heal the earth
    also,
Death, in your time.

Jeffers, like the old Christian writers, always works
and sees from the dark center of his being, from the
point we call the purely subjective which is beyond
science and reason. This centralization or deracina-
tion of the unconscious is called by the Chinese *Tao*,
that which is outside of mathematical truth and time.
The Upanishadic *Demiurgus* is the same eternal actu-
ation of the dark-self breaking out into the vast not-
self, the universal. To Boehme this was "seeing with
philosophic eyes." To Blake it was the "double vision."
This seeing from the dark center of one's being is not
a pessimistic nor an optimistic outlook as regards earthly things; it is the Nietzschean road beyond good and
evil.

Perhaps if we can imagine the poet Jeffers as Hae-
phestus doing his shining work from the volcanic fires
of his own being, in his underworld cave, we shall
understand why Jeffers speaks so often of fire and darkness, and why in his poetry there is so much "shining."

This brings us to the most specific and vital symbol
in all Jeffers's work—fire. The Vedic *Hymns* say,
"The head of Heaven, the navel of Earth, is Agni"
(fire). Fire is the earthly form of heavenly light; the
infant Zarathustra was taken out of fire. In the Bible
God is "a consuming fire," the active masculine principle. "Before there was water there was fire."

In *Roan Stallion* Jeffers writes: "Humanity is the mold to break away from, the crust to break through, the coal to break into fire," and also, "Figures and symbols, castlings of fire, played in her brain; but the white fire was the essence."

George Sterling in his *Robinson Jeffers, the Man and the Artist,* tells us that Jeffers does not believe in punishment nor in the taking of human or animal life. Even the trees are sacred to him:

> He had bared his knife-blade to cut the bough, en-
>   during her voice, but Fera
> Caught the raised wrist. "Let it be. We have no right.
> The trees are decent, but we! A redwood cut
> To make the coffin, an oak's roots for the grave: some
>   day the coast will lost patience and dip
> And be clean . . . . "

He feels even with the humble lobster:

> She sunned herself by the fire,
> Watching with fascinated speculation of pain
> The antennae of lobsters like spikes of jointed grass
> Above the heating water in a five-gallon tin
> Writhe at the sky, lives unable to scream.

The over-sensitive psyche of the poet takes upon itself the pain of *Hurt Hawks:*

> The broken pillar of the wing jags from the clotted
>   shoulder,
> The wing trails like a banner in defeat,
> No more to use the sky forever but live with famine

And pain a few days: cat nor coyote
Will shorten the week of waiting for death, there is
    game without talons.
He stands under the oak-bush and waits
The lame feet of salvation; at night he remembers
    freedom
And flies in a dream, the dawn ruins it.
He is strong and pain is worse to the strong, in-
    capacity is worse.
The curs of the day come and torment him
At distance, no one but death the redeemer will hum-
    ble that head,
The intrepid readiness, the terrible eyes.
The wild God of the world is sometimes merciful to
    those
That ask mercy, not often to the arrogant.
You do not know him, you communal people, or you
    have forgotten him;
Intemperate and savage, the hawk remembers him;
Beautiful and wild, the hawks, and men that are dy-
    ing, remember him.

As the above poem shows, one of Jeffers's favorite
animal symbols in the hawk. Another is the horse. To
Plato the horse was the symbol of the highest aspect
of the human intellect. In his *Republic* he wrote:
"Then how can he, who has magnificence of mind and
is the spectator of all time and all existence, think much
of human life? He cannot. Nor can such an one account death fearful? No indeed." In the *Stapatha
Brahmana* we read: "He addressed the horse with

'thus born art thou, a child of the two worlds.' " And again: "Man does not rightly know the way to the heavenly world, but the horse does." We are all familiar with Pegasus of the Greek poets, who, to Jeffers is "the dark strength." We shuddered, too, at the spectral white horses of Ibsen's *Rosmersholm,* rushing forth in the darkness, in the silence.

In *Roan Stallion* California, the woman, prayed aloud to the horse, "O God, I am not good enough, O Fear, O Strength . . . O clean Power". The Indians had their phallic stallion, Mamoji, to touch which caused maidens to bear children. A menstruating woman was kept in seclusion so that "she might not approach nor touch a horse," for the Indians believed that "such contamination" would impoverish or weaken the animal. In Jeffers's poem a menstruating woman is involved, hence the tragic conflict:

> Crying in her mind, she fired three times before the
>   haunches crumpled sidewise, the fore-legs stif-
>   fening,
> And the beautiful strength settled to earth; she turned
>   then on her little daughter the mask of a woman
> Who has killed God.

D. H. Lawrence interprets the horse symbol thus: "Horses, always horses, as a symbol he roams the dark underworld meadows of the soul. He stamps and threshes in the dark fields of your soul and mine. With the last fifty years man has lost the horse. Now man is lost. Man is lost to life and power; an underling and wastrel, the horse the symbol of surging potency and power of movement, of action, in man."

In *St. Mawr* Lawrence, employing what Edmund Wilson calls "the principles of symbolism in fiction," uses the stallion, as does Jeffers, for the Aryan symbol of god-like strength, freedom in action, power, and immortality. In Lawrence's story as in Jeffers's poem, man has become the breaker of natural laws, the "sublimated life-essences" of Spengler. The irruption of the physical is beginning to break into the spiritual life of the protagonist. In both cases it is rather an attack than a surrender to the complete downfall of the moral forces in the individual beyond his will. Lawrence's Lou is suffering inertia from eunuchoid man (over-civilization and mechanism of the human); the body of the stallion, St. Mawr, "glowing red with power," becomes to her "a splendid demon and she must worship him." For a time she finds the male virginity-power in the stallion, but toward the end of the story the horse succumbs to the attractions of a mare, and the tale ends as an ironic study of iconolagny.

Where Lawrence's novel ends, Jeffers's poem begins. Lawrence symbolizes in the stallion the dark human passion, the ithyphallic god; Jeffers, the shining god-power, *potentia*. This shining god-power is always killed by men for the thing they love more—physical passion; thus Jeffers's poem ends tragically.

The difference between Lou and California is psychological rather than logical. In a way it explains the message of the two poets—for Lawrence was at heart a poet. They awaken spiritual revaluation of the human will-to-power. Granville Hicks in *The Great Tradition* explains Jeffers's use of symbolism in situations such as the above: "Jeffers chooses his events, not because they are representative in any statistical sense, but because they do symbolize what seem to him the significant and revealing moments of human life." He gives us "humanity at stricken moments," losing itself and finding itself through doubt or the experience called by the orthodox sin.

It is difficult to explain or describe the primary inspiration, the brazen boldness and lofty exaltation, of the ancient stallion symbol in modern literature. It must of course be freed from the narrowness of its obscurantism through theology and superstition. It is a symbol, resurrected in the modern psyche, of extreme earth-consciousness. A very recent appearance of this stallion symbol in present-day literature is in Jack Lindsay's novel, *The Lady and the Mute,* a first novel by a young Englishman. He writes: "People must feel . . . must imagine, must see suffering . . . and understand it and take it upon themselves," in order to break away from it. The mute Chisnell is left alone with the stallion, which has taken vengeance for him upon his enemy. " 'Oh, beautiful body,' his heart cried, and his own body became the bearer of all the crude animal strength and desire and the crudest sex which was in the horse."

The Gallinomeros of California have this legend, according to Bancroft: "The hawk flew in the coyote's face in the primeval darkness, apologies ensued, and the pair together made the sun." Homer called hawks the "swift messengers of Phoebus." The Egyptians often represented the soul of man by the hawk. The Egyptian *bak* (hawk) was the emblem of Horus, the rising sun. Angelo de Gubernatis in his *Zoological Mythology* tells us that among primitive peoples "the hawk is sometimes nailed on the doors of stables for good luck."

Among Jeffers's many references to hawks and other birds the most beautiful and the most highly symbolic and philosophic is the passage in *Cawdor* referring to the flight of the captive eagle's spirit:

> It saw from the height and desert space of unbreath-
> able air
> Where meteors make green fire and die, the ocean
> dropping westward to the girdle of the pearls of
> dawn
> And the hinder edge of the night sliding toward
> Asia; it saw far under eastward the April-
> delighted
> Continent; and time relaxing about it now, abstracted
> from being, it saw the eagles destroyed,

Mean generations of gulls and crows taking their
    world; turn for turn in the air, as on earth
The white faces drove out the brown. It saw the white
    decayed and the brown from Asia returning;
It saw men learn to outfly the hawk's brood and forget
    it again; it saw men cover the earth and again
Devour each other and hide in caverns, be scarce as
    wolves. It neither wondered nor cared, and it saw
Growth and decay alternate forever, and the tides
    returning.

It saw, according to the sight of its kind, the archetype
Body of life a beaked carniverous desire
Self-upheld on storm-broad wings; but the eyes
Were spouts of blood; the eyes were gashed out; dark
    blood
Ran from the ruinous eye-pits to the hook of the beak
And rained on the waste spaces of heaven.
Yet the great Life continued; yet the great Life
Was beautiful, and she drank her defeat, and de-
    voured her famine for food.

There the eagle's phantom perceived
Its prison and its wound were not its peculiar wretch-
    edness,
All that lived was maimed and bleeding, caged or in
    blindness,
Lopped at the ends with death and conception, and
    shrewd
Cautery of pain on the stumps to stifle the blood, but
    not
Refrains for all that; life was more than its functions

And accidents, more important than its pains and
    pleasures,
A torch to burn in with pride, a necessary
Ecstasy in the run of the cold substance,
The scape-goat of the greater world. (But as for me,
I have heard the summer dust crying to be born
As much as ever flesh cried to be quiet.)
Pouring itself on fulfilment the eagle's passion
Left life behind and flew at the sun, its father.
The great unreal talons took peace for prey
Exultantly, their death beyond death; stooped upward
    and struck
Peace like a white fawn in a dell of fire.

Seen from the heights of the far-reaching eyes of
the eagle, our mundane planet might look as it did to
Dante's Heavenly Eagle, which dared to fix his eyes
upon the full-blazing sun.

Intuitively considered, the eagle through "Self-annihilation" has become to Jeffers the source and "gran-
deur of Inspiration."

In the strength and beauty of the above passage we
find the poet's spiritualized focus or *Weltauschauung*
of his whole nature realized or lifted up in a transfig-
ured reality where earthly life has become an alien
"vision shadowy of Truth." The poet here has cast a
final seal of approbation upon the imaginative powers
of his genius.

Some of us might recall the Spanish-American poet,
Ruben Dario's, *Salutacion Al Aquila* written in 1906 to

welcome the North-American delegates to the Pan-American Congress held in Brazil; the poet has some superb lines of lyric sweep. It opens with a salute to the magic eagle, symbolizing the spirit of Whitman:—

> Bie Vengas, oh mágica Aquila, que amara tanto
> Walt Whitman

As the eagle ascends upon the rhythmic scale of the poem, the world, as in Jeffers's poem, seems less and less important:—

> Es incidencia la Historia. Nuestro destino supremo
> está más del rumbo que marcan fugaces las épocas.
>
> *   *   *   *   *   *   *
>
> Aquila prodigiosa, que te nutres de luz y de azual,
> como un cruz viviente, vuela sore estas naciones,
> Y comunica al globo la victoria feliz del futuro!

D. H. Lawrence's *Eagle in New Mexico* beginning:

> Towards the sun, towards the south west
> A scorched breast.
> A scorched breast, breasting the sun like an answer.

should be accepted as the embodiment of Lawrence's own individual self—strong in solid singleness.

Before taking up sex and erotic symbolism as Jeffers uses them in his work, let us refer to Havelock Ellis: "The phenomena of erotic symbolism can scarcely fail to be profoundly impressive to the patient and impartial student of the human soul. They often seem absurd, sometimes disgusting, occasionally criminal. They are always, when carried to an extreme, abnormal. But of all the manifestations of sexual psychology, normal or abnormal, they are the most specifically human. More than any others, they involve the potently plastic force of the imagination. They constitute the supreme triumph of human idealism."

Male, according to Buddhistic doctrine, is form, female matter; male the sun, female the moon. "For the moon herself, out of desire for the sun, revolves around and comes in contact with him because she loves to derive from him the generative power," says Plutarch. Osiris, the male, becomes involved in matter, the female, in order to rise in greater shining during the emanation (morning). "And the Lord God caused a deep sleep to fall upon the man"—*Genesis* II: 21-23. In the *Buddha Karita* we read: "Verily the life of woman is always darkness."

From all this we gather Jeffers's symbolic conception of woman as used in his longer tragic poems. Man has become to Jeffers the Nietzschean "woman's natural prey." To man she is no longer the Homeric Athena, the Socratic Diotima, the Dantesque *donna de la mia mente,* the Goethean *ewigweibliche.* Jeffers's women are primitives, Amazon types such as Keyserling describes "who believe in facts only, lead sex lives such as the most immoral of males, provided he has a soul, would never lead." Woman has become ashes of desire

for Jeffers's men—self-seeking, self-perverted Eves, Cly-
temnestras, Messalinas, Medeas, of modern civilization.
Through her man has lost his fire and has become an
introvert—a passionate enemy of materialism and, in
his own way, a passionate believer in the solace of nature—nature, which he knows to be greater than himself, above humanity. He has learned to perceive, as
Spinoza calls it, "from the aspect of eternity."

An erotic symbol used by Jeffers which has been a
stumbling block to the understanding of many readers
is incest. The word incest fills us today with horror and
loathing. But the world has not always so considered it.
Freud writes: "Mythology teaches that incest, apparently so abhorred by men, is permitted to the gods
without further thought, and you may learn from
ancient history that incestuous marriage with his sister was holy prescript for the person of the ruler." By
incest Jeffers symbolizes the life of humanity "turned
inward," seeking only itself, and this it must break
away from:

> You have walked in a dream, consumed with your
>   fathers and your mothers, you have loved
> Inside the four walls of humanity; passions turned
>   inward, incestuous desires, and a fighting against
>   ghosts.

To Jeffers the figure of the Christ stands for the age-
old quietism of the East, and also for a symbol of the

tortured introvert in humanity's troublous journey through life:

> I saw my future when I was with God; but now at
>   length in a flashing moment the means: I fright-
>   fully
> Lifted up drawing all men to my feet: I go a stranger
>   passage to a greater dominion,
> More tyrannous, more terrible, more true, than Caesar
>   or any other subduer of the earth before him has
>   dared to dream of

Again, in *Point Pinos and Point Lobos,* Jeffers speaks of Christ:

> I am not among the mockers, Master, I am one of
>   your lovers,
> Ah weariest spirit in all the world, we all have rest
> Being dead but you still strive, nearly two thousand
>   years
> You have wrestled for us against God . . .

If this is not faith, then what is faith? Jeffers's faith is like that of Dostoievsky, a faith in "the progressive renewal of man, the story of his slow transformation, of his passage from one world to another, of the discovery which he has made of a new and hitherto unknown reality." Of course to a Michael Gold, whose theory of poetry is that it "should be useful" for communistic propaganda, Jeffers would answer "is humanity worthy to be under that lightning?" or:

Remember always that dreams are deceivers,
No one's exempt from dreaming,
Not even I. But all's fraud, fragments of thought
Fitting themselves together without a mind.

To Jeffers, God, the First Mind, speaks through action. Action means the realization of the not-self in the cosmos, growth, harmony, as distinguished from the activity of the individual who has become "slavish in the mass." "The actual mass man is, in fact, a primitive who has slipped through the wings of the age-old stage of civilization"; who lives now "with our technical requirements, but not by them," says Jose Ortegna y'Gasset in his *Revolt of the Masses*. The poet's "business is with action, not with the result of action." God is also peace dwelling in Nirvana, and to worship him we must be worshippers of the One-ness of this pantheistic "God without name, God without form, the Lord of Asia . . . here as there." One of Jeffers's most profoundly religious passages begins:

                              Serenely smiling
Face of the godlike man made God, who tore the web
    of human passions
As a yellow lion the antelope-hunter's net, and freeing
    himself made free
All who could follow, the tissue of new births and
    deaths dissolved away from him,
He reunited with the passionless light sky, not again to
    suffer

The shame of the low female gate, freed, never to be
    born again,
Whom Maha Maya bore in the river garden, the
    Himalayan barrier northward
Bounding the world: is it freedom, smile of the Budd-
    ha, surely freedom? For someone
Whispered into my ear when I was very young, some
    serpent whispered
That what has gone returns, nothing shall stop nor
    destroy it, we are bound on the wheel,
We and the stars and seas, the mountains and the
    Buddha. Weary tidings
To cross the weary, bitter to bitter men: life's con-
    queror will not fear
Life; and to meditate again under the sacred tree, and
    again
Vanquish desire will be no evil.

Jeffers does not employ a coined symbolism as Blake
does, nor does he invest private mythologies with special meanings. He uses the oldest and most primitive
world symbols. Present-day thought has certainly
made, in some ways, a fetish of ancient symbolism,
mythology, primitive beliefs. Spengler's monumental
Decline of the West is filled with such allusions, so is
The Magic Mountain of Thomas Mann, so is Proust,
so are the works of Freud, Jung, and the living philosophers; even in politics we hark back to Plato's Republic. Jeffers, with his mental eye on the dim past
and his inward eye on the unborn future, is a citizen
of this shining but perishing republic. A Marxist writ-
er or poet or painter can doubtless find real support in

the theory of his class; but Jeffers living in an epoch
when, as Lunacharsky says, "the classes are beginning
to decay, having no ideology, having no hope of main-
taining their dominance," turns to no class, leaves humanity out, and returns to "the never-failing principle
of joy"—nature.

J. C. Powys has characterized this inhuman or super-
human level by calling it that of the "ichthyosaurus
ego." It is a state at once above and below the so-called
natural level of man's life. It leads back to a primordial existence, the state called by Jacob Boehme the
super-sensual, or the "life above sense," where the human ego is annihilated in a pananthropistic god and
finds panacea only in a nature god.

In poetry we are likely to find frequent use of the
word "shining." This shining wonder must be the joyful wisdom of life under the sun—in the mystic poets
the joy that sees beyond mere seeing, the "white radiance of eternity." Jeffers calls to the poets of the past
across the centuries of their meditations:

> Far-flown ones, you children of the hawks, dream fu-
>   ture when you lean from a crag of the last planet
>   or the ocean
> Of the stars, remember we also have known beauty.

Some of his most significant references to death we
find in Jeffers's sixteen elegiac poems, *Descent to the
Dead*. One of these, *Inscription for a Gravestone,* is so
outstanding that it should be quoted *in toto*:

I am not dead, I have only become inhuman:
That is to say,
Undressed myself of laughable prices and infirmities,
But not as a man
Undresses to creep into bed, but like an athlete
Stripping for the race.
The delicate ravel of nerves that made me a measurer
Of certain fictions
Called good and evil; that made me contract with pain
And expand with pleasure;
Fussily adjusted like a little electroscope:
That's gone, it is true;
(I never miss it; if the universe does,
How easily replaced!)
But all the rest is heightened, widened, set free.
I admired the beauty
While I was human, now I am a part of the beauty.
I wander in the air,
Being mostly gas and water, and flow in the ocean;
Touch you and Asia
At the same moment; have a hand in the sunrises
And the glow of this grass.
I left the light precipitate of ashes to earth
For a love-token.

It is evident from reading the citations we have made
from Jeffers's poetry that he possesses something which
the modern psyche has lost—lost as Orpheus lost his
Eurydice, perhaps forever. There is nothing of the con-
ventional "Spoon River" conception of death in Jeffers's poems. As are all things to him, Death, too, is a
part of his mystic conception of the descent of man.

The upward and downward trends, the ever increasing complexity of the animate world, man's awareness of himself as a part of the scheme, are all here. It is a reply to Goethe's question as to how anthropomorphic a man really is. The Egyptians show the same conception of death in their *Book of the Dead,* the Greeks in the Orpheus myth and in their belief in Tartarian darkness beneath the earth, and in the Lethean waters of oblivion. Christ meant this in "before Abraham was, I am," as did the early Christians in the *descensus Christi.* We have lost the Dark Mother, that prelogical, instinctive reaction to nature which Keats calls "the negative capability." "The world is too much with us," and this subtle, psychophysical fusion of man's nature with the earth, the *deus sive natura* of Spinoza, is gone for us. But Jeffers the poet feels it intensely.

St. Francis expiring, lying naked on the earth, had this earth-consciousness. Sir Thomas Browne had it when he wrote *Urn Burial.* Shakespeare has expressed it in *Hamlet* and *The Tempest.* In Nietzsche's "from you, my dearest dead ones, cometh unto me a sweet savor, heart-opening and melting," we see it. Blake says: "I will go down to the sepulchre to see if morning breaks." Wordsworth found "the human soul of universal earth, dreaming of things to come," Shelley in *Adonais* says: "Clasp with thy panting soul the pendulous earth." To Keats it was the longed-for "draught of vintage that hath been cool'd a long age

in the deep delved earth." Such a belief leads to a pantheistic communion with immortality, a new spiritual
birth regenerated from death, through losing the self
and finding the self; it is a primitive inheritance, an
intuition; it has as little in common with reason as
theology with religion. It must be approached with
Blakean "private judgment"; it affects the particular
individual only in his own psyche, especially the poetic
psyche, where "the living dream, but the dead are
awake," and where "one thousand years will hardly
leach . . . this dust of that fire."

PART IV

TRAGEDY: AN APPROACH TO THE NOT-SELF

I stir up your pure minds by
way of remembrance.
II Peter 3-1

I must be cruel, only to be
kind.
Shakespeare

TRAGEDY: AN APPROACH TO THE NOT-SELF

L ET us refresh our memories by reviewing the origin of dramatic tragedy in ancient ritualistic worship of the dead. The word is derived from the Greek τράγος, he-goat, and ὀιδός, singer, hence τραγωδία, tragedy. The lyric dithyramb was sung by a male chorus clad in goat-skins during religious rites in honor of Dionysus, adding, as it were, the earthly sacrificial element to the dramatic song. A later attribute added to the idea of tragedy was the moralistic conception of the Greek Μοιρὰ, or Fate-idea, which governs all the great Grecian dramatists. In the belief of the Greeks, Fate ruled even the Gods. "Awful is the mysterious power of Fate," wrote Sophocles.

Aristotle defines tragedy as "imitation of an action." This "action" forces itself upon man when he interferes with the fixity of Fate, or the will of God, which is beyond human will. This fixity of Fate as related to human destiny is a kind of preordained necessity. If man does not obey this necessity, Fate destroys him. Such destruction is tragedy.

The modern mind demands a more specifically poetic or imaginative conception than the traditionally accepted definitions afford. Robinson Jeffers has given us this; he has found the tragic note in modern American life. With deep intuition and vivid imagination, working through an extremely individual and original poetic temperament, he sees and proclaims the total failure, spiritually, of modern values. Aristotle's poetic and aesthetic pleasures in contemplating tragic "imitations of action" become to a mind like Jeffers's in Shelley's words:

> "the ministers of pain and fear,
> And disappointment, and mistrust and hate
> And clinging crime"

To Jeffers tragedy is the oldest form "under which the mind may most clearly and freely contemplate the human situation," may challenge the ruinous present-day conditions and facts of an every-day life the tragic consequences of which surpass those noble but episodic calamities resulting from the struggle of humanity against Fate. Perhaps Jeffers's "tremendous image" of tragedy, the Hegelian "cosmic justice" and Freud's "death instinct," may best be summarized in the phrase of Nietzsche as "the dissolution of the individual and his unification with primordial existence." Once we realize this "cosmic justice," this destroyer and preserver of all we deem worth while in our lives, we cannot calmly be

> Contented to think that everything has been done
> That's in the scope of the race; so should I also perhaps
> Dream, under the empty angel of this twilight,
> But the great memory of that inhumanized world,

With all its wave of good and evil to climb yet,
Its exorbitant power to match, its heartless passion to
    equal,
And all its music to make, beats on the grave-mound.

Jeffers's "Denmark" is a continent; "Elsinore," the
stone tower built by Jeffers's own hands at Carmel on
the California coast; for Hamlet's soliloquy substitute
our poet's:

This coast crying out for tragedy like all beautiful
    places,
(The quiet ones ask for quieter suffering; but here the
    granite cliff the gaunt cypresses crown
Demands what victim? The dykes of red lava and
    black what Titan? The hills like pointed flames
Beyond Soberanes, the terrible peaks of the bare hills
    under the sun, what immolation?)
This coast crying out for tragedy like all beautiful
    places: and like the passionate spirit of humanity
Pain for its bread: God's, many victims', the painful
    deaths, the horrible transfigurements: I said in my
    heart,
"Better invent than suffer: imagine victims
Lest your own flesh be chosen agonist, or you
Martyr some creature to the beauty of the place."

In this poem called *Apology for Bad Dreams* we see
Jeffers as the tragic poet of modern America. What to
Athanasius was divinity, to Jeffers is nature—nature
and divinity always separated from humanity. It is
when the natural in humanity is crushed out by materialism that evil enters and tragedy begins. It strikes

home to Jeffers as it did to Hamlet that "the time is out of joint"; we "must break out of humanity." Tragedy

> breaks man's face and a white fire flies out of it;
>   vision that fools him
> Out of his limits, desire that fools him out of his
>   limits, unnatural crime, inhuman science,
> Slit eyes in the mask; wild loves that leap over the
>   walls of nature, the wild fence-vaulter science,
> Useless intelligence of far stars, dim knowledge of the
>   spinning demons that make an atom,
> These break, these pierce, these deify, praising their
>   God shrilly with fierce voices: not in a man's
>   shape
> He approves the praise, he that walks lightning-naked
>   on the Pacific, that laces the suns with planets,
> The heart of the atom with electrons: what is human-
>   ity in this cosmos? For him, the last
> Least taint of a trace in the dregs of the solution; for
>   itself, the mold to break away from, the coal
> To break into fire, the atom to be split.

The tragedies of Jeffers are fatal events, beyond good and evil, in which human lives are lost "by unauthorized violence." They are not tragedies in any Aristotelian "imitation of noble actions." Rather, primitive instincts still ruling humanity in the twentieth century, are the source of the tragic events in Jeffers's longer poems. He believes with Plato that "madness like vice must be known but not practised or imitated." To avoid hard realities, to save ourselves through illusion, to try to be happy in deluding ourselves, or in con-

sidering evil only as "bad dreams," is not Jeffers's
gospel. "It is strange enough," to quote Nietzsche,
"that the association of lust, religion and cruelty did not
long ago draw men's attention to their close relationship and common tendency." The every day cruelties
many of us still believe and accept only as bad dreams
out of a mad poet's brain. Aeschylus too felt like Jeffers that neither the payment of blood money nor the
performance of rituals could quiet the conscience or
carry civilization very far. Jeffers the poet, being a
person whose sensibilities are very sharply attuned to
pain in the world, could not fail to suffer intensely
when facing realities such as war, torture of animals
by man, torture of man himself by "nature's cruel
holiness," as Blake has named his pananthropic god.
Like a doctor or surgeon laboring to diagnose disease
and expose sores in order to cure them, Jeffers strives
with the blight of evil caused by blind egotism and
human perversions and degradations:

> for what are we,
> The beast that walks upright, with speaking lips
> And little hair, to think we should always be fed,
> Sheltered, intact, and self-controlled? We sooner more
> > liable
> Than the other animals. Pain and terror, the insanities
> > of desire; not accidents, but essential,
> And crowd up from the core.

Jeffers sees and feels for humanity both love and
hatred. He has the same pity for humanity as he would

have for a blind person or a wounded animal. He knows, with Herbert Spencer, that "all evil is the result of non-adaptation and continually changing constitutions. . . . Man needed one moral constitution to fit him for his original state; he needs another to fit him for his present state; and he has been, is, and will long continue to be in process of adaptation." Jeffers reflects the image of Nietzsche's "ugliest man," the modern barbarian of this generation. We have lived too long upon invented suffering and imagined victims. "A man having bad dreams who invents victims, is only the ape of God."

The dramatists, the writers of fiction, the magazines, supply us, day in and day out, with invented pain. We have grown callous to actual cruelty. Many of us do not know it exists round the corner, do not recognize it in our midst. We have become intellectually strabismic; our eyes have been turned too long inward, upon ourselves, not toward the cosmic not-self. The "monstrous hardness" which some readers find in Nietzsche and Jeffers is the result of great misunderstanding, as has already been shown in the case of the latter by his poem *Hurt Hawks* and other quotations. Nietzsche explains this "defensive instinct become hard" from his own experience: "I am perpetually remaking the same mistake—overestimating others; suffering from childhood onwards, I have had repeated confirmation of the truth that to feel compassion was the greatest of my dangers."

In his *Confessions* St. Augustine states: "All things that are corrupted are deprived of good. But if they are deprived of all good, they will cease to exist. In so far as they exist, they are good. Evil is no substance."

The problem of the nature of evil has never ceased to occupy the minds of humanitarians. Milton admitted "evil into the mind of God or man." Jeffers sees evil as something positive, a disruption of forces making in the end for a deeper orientation of good in the human psyche. Jeffers, as does Euripides, reflects the feelings of a changeful epoch in an outgrown culture that is gradually disappearing. He himself is a genuine offspring of our age of transition. The lower, more undeveloped side of human nature has never before been treated more realistically in poetry than by Jeffers. The many small details and trifling circumstances and incidents of daily living are used to give deeper reality to his representation. The realism and verity with which Jeffers depicts scenes of violent and uncontrollable emotion have never been surpassed in modern poetry. Although he pictures the outward effects of mental suffering, his tragic victims—"giants in agony"—are not driven by any outward fate, but by the evil suggestions and desires of their own blind natures.

Sex, suicide and insanity are the three brutal agents most frequently employed by the Greek, Elizabethan and many modern playwrights to create the tragic catastrophe. With Jeffers death becomes the symbol of the actual dying of an outworn social, moral or ethical order of civilization, as with the Russian writers before the Revolution swept away Russian culture. Tolstoy, Dostoievsky and Gorky are the painters of ugly pictures of Russian humanity—humanity in the amorphous state with distorted types such as Daumier painted. Yet how far removed from, how deep and true by comparison, are even the most realistic of Jeffers's poems, from this bit of anti-harmonics from the 'windy cithern' of Wallace Stevens's mind:

> The world, a turnip once so readily plucked,
> Sacked up and carried over seas, daubed out
>   Of its ancient purple, pruned to the fertile main,
> And sown again by the stiffest realist,
> Came reproduced in purple, family font,
> The same insoluble lump.

The above stanza is as typical as any of the effortless camouflage of a pseudo-poetic mind, yet what wasted craft and oil of the Dada-Stein studio lamp is behind the dusty idiosyncrasies of the meretricious Waste-landers. Jeffers's reply to our clever vice producers is:

> Spirited people make a thousand jewels in verse and
>   prose, and the restlessness of talent
> Runs over and floods the stage or spreads its fever on
>   canvas.
> They are skilled in music too, the demon is never sat-
>   isfied, they take to puppets, they invent

New arts, they take to drugs . . . and we all applaud
    our vices.
Mine, coldness and the tenor of a stone tranquillity;
    slow life, the growth of trees and verse,
Content the unagitable and somewhat earth-fast
    nature.

The human mind never comes to an understanding of itself until it has understood the *katharsis* of the tragic sorrow in the vast cosmos, the not-self. It is almost the uncompromisingly realistic faith of Tolstoy's religion of action, not prayer; a religion that "takes us by the shoulders and gives us a vigorous push forwards."

The late Prof. George B. Foster of the University of Chicago has made very clear the significance of classic Greek tragedy: "The strength of mind and body which reveals itself in the ability to contemplate the sufferings of life as being necessary to the creation of beauty can be the privilege of but few. The Greeks considered the sight of suffering and of pain as adding to the value and to the beauty of life. They contemplated suffering and pain in the light of an aesthetic manifestation of the Universal Will, of which all life is but a manifestation. After enjoying the sublimity of the Olympian vision of the beauty, the strength, and the eternity of life, the Greeks liked to renew their vigor by going once more to the source of life, which is suffering."

Before we approach Jeffers's poetic tragedies, let us remind ourselves that we must deal with him as with other original poets—that is, with suspended judgment, conjectures, and comparisons; not with fact-knowledge nor criticism such as was directed against Blake and Shelley. Some of the English critics found in Shelley "low pride, cold selfishness and unmanly cruelty."

We shall study Jeffers's tragic poems in the chronological order of their publication, keeping in mind Arthur Little's paradox of art, "The communication of immoral experience may be means to moral elevation."

Roan Stallion is, according to one reviewer writing in 1926, "an unforgettable and thoroughly unpleasant performance." Literal and natural enough reaction! Taken literally, *Roan Stallion* is the story of a woman in love with a horse her husband has bought. California, the woman, "erect and strong as a new tower, only a fourth part Indian," has known her husband and other men only sexually. She has looked upon her lascivious husband, Johnny, "for years with neither love nor loathing." Suddenly she awakens to a new spiritual love for a clean, powerful, beautiful being—a nature god, symbolized in the great stallion. We see in this highly symbolic poem how fully and deeply Jeffers penetrates the dark, primitive psyche of the woman, California, who might be a symbol of the California coast "crying out for tragedy like all beautiful places." The woman senses in the stallion a power long dead in herself and her husband—the psychic communion of true lovers. The *anima mundi,* or vital force of her being, strives to reach love in outer nature:

> She prayed aloud: "O god, I am not good enough;
> O fear, O strength, I am draggled.
> Johnny and other men have had me, and O clean
> power!
> Here am I," she said, falling before him.

Perhaps the Dane, Dirk Coster, has refined Freud's original explanation of this exaggerated love of animals: "It is an innate hate and it is a hate born of disappointment; the hate which is shown directly in love of animals is inhuman, sombre and mysterious. There is stored up a secret pain and a secret thirst; the longing to be able to enjoy, in the relation with these creatures of nature, at least a fugitive draught of pure, spiritual disinterested love for which the soul, in spite of everything, is doomed to yearn."

In his poem Jeffers shows clearly that we cannot objectify ourselves nor emerge outward from the dark center without deep suffering, often without the "bloodsacrifice" of some one else; "God's many victims; the painful deaths, the horrible transfigurements." In shooting the stallion the woman killed in her own mind "the phantom rulers of humanity that, without being, are yet more real than what they are born of." In other words, she killed her sensations making for regeneration.

In *The Tower beyond Tragedy,* Jeffers's greatest
work, he imitates the Greek drama, even deserting his
California scene and laying his plot in Mycenae. The
poem opens with Agamemnon's home-coming after
the fall of Troy. His wife, Clytemnestra, sister of Hel-
en, greets him. Among his captives Agamemnon has a
princess, Cassandra, the daughter of Priam and Hecu-
ba. This Cassandra is cursed with the power of prophecy, given to her by Apollo. She foresaw the downfall of Troy and all the misfortunes of the race. Jeffers
transforms her in the latter half of his tragedy into the
avenging spirit of the murdered Agamemnon, whose
soul takes possession of Cassandra's body and speaks
through it. In revenge for the immolation of her sister's daughter, Iphigenia, Clytemnestra kills Agamemnon while he is bathing within the palace. Aegisthus,
in whose care the king had left his house and family,
has proved to be unfaithful to his trust, having made
Clytemnestra his mistress and usurped the throne. Clytemnestra and Aegisthus are slain by Orestes and Electra after the murder of their father. Orestes is driven
insane by the Furies and Electra hangs herself.

The above is a mere skeleton outline of the plot.
After the murder of their mother and Aegisthus, Electra demands that her brother mount the throne to
which he is the rightful heir. Then he confesses to his
sister his incestuous desires—Jeffers's symbol of "racial
introversion." When Electra declares herself willing

to submit to his unholy passion, or to kill herself to cure his madness, Orestes flees to the mountains, discarding forever humanity and all human attributes to lose himself in the life of the elements. In his "breaking away from humanity," Jeffers contrasts him with Electra, the woman, to whom the house, family, her native city and country, are sacred. The family instinct as it appears in her, who is devoid even of race feeling, is on the animal level. The same weaknesses as those of her mother, Clytemnestra, Orestes finds in his sister, so he flees from her and all human kind, saying

> We shall never ascend this mountain.
> So it might come true: we have to be tough against
>   them,
> Our dreams and visions, or they true themselves into
>   flesh. It is sweet: I faint for it: the old stones here
> Have seen more and not moved.   A custom of the
>   house. To accept you, little Electra, and go my
>   journey
> Tomorrow: you'd call cheating. Therefore: we shall
>   not go up this mountain, dearest, dearest,
> Tonight nor ever. It's Cyltemnestra in you. But the
>   dead are a weak tribe. If I had Agamemnon's
> We'd live happily, sister, and lord it in Mycenae—be a
>   king like the others—royalty and incest
> Run both in the stream of the blood.

Orestes was later purged and freed from his narrow personal self through the tragic experience of his madness. In order to attain cosmic consciousness and forget the pitiable self-love innate in love of parents, sister and home, he breaks away from it all. Beyond mere personal ends, he at last finds adjustment in universal life. At the end of life nothing is really destroyed; death is only dissolution into primitive elements, which are the fountain source of all life.

Not since Swinburne's *Erechtheus* and *Atalanta* has a tragic poem of such height, depth and power been written. Shakespeare's line, "the proud, full sail of his great verse," is suggested by passages like the following:

> Few years or many signified less than nothing
> To him who has climbed the tower beyond time,
>   consciously, and cast humanity, entered the earlier
>   fountain.

The scholarly reader will perceive that, in *The Tower beyond Tragedy,* Jeffers has employed a forcefulness and directness of style typical of the great Greek dramatists. His lines are as cruel as Maenads driven mad by Dionysus and attacking Pentheus with flaming torches and pointed thyrsi. In this poetic tragedy he has restored and built from broken fragments a new classic temple with sacrificial flame rising from forgotten altars and burning with that "hard, gemlike flame to maintain this ecstasy—this almost barbaric ecstasy of the Greek spirit with its harmonies, storms, victories, of the unseen and intellectual world, which, wrought out into bodily form, give it an interest and significance communicable to it alone."

Take for instance this word-painting from the opening of the poem at the king's home-coming:

> This Clytemnestra was her sister, low-statured, fierce-
>   lipped, not dark nor blond, greenish-gray-eyed,
> Sinewed with strength, you saw, under the purple
>   folds of the queen-cloak, but craftier than queenly,
> Standing between the gilded wooden porch-pillars,
>   great steps of stone above the steep street,
> Awaiting the King.

And

> He raised his thick burnt-colored beard and smiled;
>   then Clytemnestra,
> Gathering the robe, setting the golden-sandalled feet
>   carefully stone by stone, descended
> One half the stair.

The Tower beyond Tragedy symbolizes the development of humanity from savagery to the "breaking-away point." This last is perhaps a fatal gesture, at least for those of us who, with Jeffers, live in spirit and sense the timeless, ever-living reality which affects powerfully our destinies in spite of the world's outer changes.

To illustrate the poet's use of intense, violent imagery, hear the murdered king's soul speak through the lips of Cassandra:

> With the voice the spirit seemed to fly out. She up-
>   flung her shining

Arms with the dreadful and sweet gesture of a woman
    surrendering utterly to force and love,
She in the eyes of the people, like a shameless woman,
    and fell writhing, and the dead King's soul
Entered her body . . . .

"Horrible things, horrible things this house has wit-
    nessed; but here is the most vile, that hundreds
Of spears are idle while the murderess, Clytemnestra
    the murderess, the snake that came upon me
Naked and bathing, the death that lay with me in bed,
    the death that has borne children to me,
Stands there unslain."

Here feeling, "the background of our deepest awareness" from the unconscious, is used as the psycho-
analysts and psychiatrists understand it. The poet
reaches the acme of awareness through the creative
power of emotion coloring perception.

As a final quotation let us take this simple but vivid
imagery; Cassandra speaks:

"O fallings of the earth: forever no rest, not forever
From the wave and the trough, from the stream and
    the slack, from growth and decay: O vulture—
Pinioned, my spirit, one flight yet, last, longest, un-
    guided,
Try into the gulf,
Over Greece, over Rome, you have space, O my spirit,
    for the years."

And this lyrical passage about that eternal snow which
science tells us will bring final peace to the earth:

> O clean, clean,
> White and most clean, colorless quietness,
> Without trace, without trail, without stain in the
>   garment drawn down
> From the poles to the girdle . . .

This gives the reader more than mere visual satisfaction for his mental eye; it gives him perception of both natural and spiritual beauty—the vision of one who has "fallen in love outward" of humanity; one to whom "few years or many signify less than nothing." It is apparent that the difference between Jeffers and Swinburne, for instance, is that the latter creates extrovertively, the former introvertively, the images of each corresponding to his own poetic temperament and conceptions. One to whom the work of Jeffers brings no revelation should never read *The Tower beyond Tragedy*. Such a reader will remain much happier in the tower of his own tragedy than beyond it. Jeffers must be understood in a single flash; in his poems, words have been made flesh, and the flesh words.

In II *Samuel* 13 we read: "Absalom, the son of David, had a fair sister whose name was Tamar, and Amnon, the son of David, loved her." Here again Jeffers chooses an old tale to symbolize the tragedy of humanity wasted inward, man regarding man exclusively, founding his desires, his values, his picture of the universe, solely upon his own race. Jeffers's *Tamar* is a story of perversion. Abnormal urges, associations and suppressions free themselves for action upon a low, unnatural plane of both mental and physical life.

In this poem Jeffers uses water—"the sweet and female sea"—as a symbol of generative power more ancient than that of blood. Lee watches his sister, Tamar, bathe:

> The murmur and splash of water made his fever fierier; something
> Unfelt before kept his eyes seaward: why should he dread to see round arm and clear throat
> Flash from the hollow stream? He trembled thinking:
> O we are beasts, a beast, what am I for?

or

> Water that owns the north and west and south
> And is all colors and never is quiet,
> And the fogs are its breath and float along the branches of the cypresses.

Tamar and her three lovers are crucified on their flesh "with the passions and lusts thereof." It is like the Platonic Table of Reason in *Phaedrus*—the eternal war between flesh and spirit, the charioteer and his steeds, the black, vicious, unruly steed of fleshly desire to be ruled by whip and spur, and the white, noble steed for which whip is not required. The poem ends like Wagner's *Gotterdammerung*—in "fire, the accepter of sacrifices, ravishing away from them their darkness."

In the same volume with *Roan Stallion* and *Tamar* is a shorter poem called *The Coast Range Christ*. It is the story of David Carrow, a "dreamer of mystical brother-hood," a coward and slacker during the world war frenzy, and of Peace O'Farrell, a Carmel farmer's wife who symbolizes blind patriotism. The poem ends with a lyrical chorus and antichorus, the former beginning:

> God was a hawk in the flow of the morning, a bee in
>   the rose that has stars for her petals,
> The far lights felt him, the first-born lamps
> Spun from the brush of his wings when he bathed in
>   the splendor of a firmament men's eyes never
>   imaged,
> Exulting in the beauty of things, a free eagle.

Perhaps it may add to the understanding of *The Women at Point Sur* if we imagine Jeffers as being in a state of mind during its writing similar to that of Ibsen while he was writing *Brand:* "At the time I wrote *Brand* I kept on my table a scorpion in a tumbler. Now and then the insect became ill. At such times I dropped into the glass a piece of soft fruit which it furiously pounced upon and injected its poison into, whereafter it became well again. Is there not a similarity between this and the writing of poetry? Natural laws are binding, even in the spiritual realm."

The Rev. Dr. Barclay, the protagonist of *The Women*

at Point Sur, is a literary type worthy to be ranked with Hamlet, Ivan Karamazov, and Brand. Dr. Barclay is a man who in the end is powerless before the unconquerable power of biological life. He may be likened to Oedipus trying to solve the riddle of the sphinx, a universal humanity seeking itself and destroyed by itself, like Hamlet in despair over the eternal fixity of things, Karamazov martyred by doubt and a great sin, Brand, bruised and bleeding, wishing "everything and nothing," eternal *Christus futurus* and *homo futurus* in conflict.

In Dr. Barclay Jeffers has created a symbol of the truth, terribly realized, that the individual cannot exist singly for himself alone, like a Lucretian atom, but is of "the mold to break away from." In this tragic poem Jeffers has touched, as does Pascal, the void outside human existence. In no other poem does his fancy reach such an eminence of unendurable height. The deep *Weltschmerz,* the blind race of man in fetters, is heroically conceived as it might have been by Michael Angelo or Beethoven. Here the Nietzschean *"Will zur Macht"* becomes, through poetic vision, a prophesy. A new note is struck—"God thinks through action"— suggesting Aquinas's "Intellectus igitur et voluntas in Deo non sunt ut potentiae, sed solum ut actiones." The Blakean "God is no more" in Jeffers has been replaced with "humanity is no more." God alone must be realized; even sacrifice of the human, the womanly, may become necessary to this realization.

When Jeffers depicts human conduct, he symbolizes, not transient human desire with its always changing objects, but the deep, instinctive tendencies of man's nature which are ever at work toward the shaping of his destiny, a process which Wordsworth calls "eternal activity without action." The greater part of humanity is human only in form, having no share in the spiritual heritage of the race. It is a "self-regardful humanity cutting itself away from the earth and the creatures, gathered home on itself, digging a pit behind it and a gulf before it."

Jeffers's *The Women at Point Sur* is like Euripides's intoxicatingly beautiful *Bacchae*—cold, sordid at one moment, soothing at another:

> I have got outside of good and evil, it needs a symbol,
> God thinks through action: when I cried on the hill,
> Love is more cruel than wolF, hungrier than flame or
>   the gape of water,
> Your virtues, your nerves, your goodness
> Rags for that fire.

Yet

> A man who can find God one moment, only one living
>   moment, has lived immortality—but how could
>   you
> Understand me?

Baffling reader and critic, thrilling with the wild, earthy music of hills, mountains, deserts, the sea, and the solitudes of the skies, Jeffers's Dionysus is disguised as a prophet standing, not before the palace at Thebes declaiming a new religion, but the Rev. Dr. Barclay preaching from a rock or

> Gathering seed in a great solitude; I shall tell you
>   everything
> When I return, but not now . . .

> He walked on the hill like one carrying a torch in the
>   wind on the hillside.

Jeffers's Dionysus is in close relationship with Demeter, Aphrodite, Eros and Apollo, who has inspired him as he did Cassandra with a prophecy of doom:

> out of me
> Destruction, out of me renewal, I preserve nothing:
>   exult with me.
> I take my chosen, I never said I would salvage you all
> Out of the net of change and renewal: they climb out
>   of the pit to the brink and suddenly they stay
> The next step with their hands: I laugh in tempests
>   over their heads in the air, and exult, and raise up
> Old violences, the mysticism, the old terror, among
>   them,
> The resurrection of time among them.

The women who follow Dr. Barclay are the Maenads, the Thyiades of Euripides, who wander with him through woods and mountains, their minds filled with priapic dreams, and the hollow sound of the ocean and the shrill notes of the wind follow them.

In addition to the "God shines through action" refrain, we find emphasized "the unconceived, the embryo before conception," and

> Annihilation, the beautiful word, the black crystal
>   structure, prisms of black crystal
> Arranged the one behind the other in the word
> To catch a ray not of this world.

Only in Blake's highly symbolic *Jerusalem* do we find the word "annihilation" used as frequently as in Jeffers's poems. By his frequent references to "annihilation" Jeffers may mean the Buddhistic following of the path of suffering to Nirvana to which, as has already been said, he so often turns:

> All the earth's agonies
> Scream in my ears like famished eaglets in the aerie
> Furious for the black flesh of annihilation . . .
> "Pain's," he said, "the foundation. I have turned to
>   love men.
> I have gathered the souls already, you've not a soul
>   among you . . . "
>
> He ran northwest, his followers
> Tired and fell off. He alone like a burnt pillar
> Smeared with the blood of sacrifice passed across the
>   black hills . . .
>
> Having not tasted water, he was dying and he said:
> I want creation. The wind over the desert
> Has turned and I will build again all that's gone down,
> I am inexhaustible.

The spiritual truth, or spiritual tragedy, or occult pleasure which Jeffers wrings out of the story of Dr. Barclay is based upon his belief that it is impossible in this life to separate matter from spirit. D. H. Lawrence must have had this same thought in mind when he wrote: "We have lost the cosmos by coming out of responsive connection with it and this is our chief tragedy." We shall seek in vain through modern poetic narratives for another Dr. Barclay in all his wildness and fantastically tragic magnificence. But in Joseph Steinbeck's poetic novel *To a God Unknown* we find the same ethnopsychology of the Druidical mind genetically and realistically present in the character of Joseph Wayne.

This is a novel written by one who understands the psychology of the earth-mystic, who has drunk from the lips of earth's impassioned clay and is not "aware of persons . . . only people" "can't see units . . . only the whole." Dr. Barclay and Wayne are in Blake's words "children of whoredom, born for sacrifice, for offering," "victims of a great delusion howling beneath the Druid's knife."

"Joseph," writes Steinbeck, "has the strength beyond vision of shattering, he has the calm of mountains, and his emotion is as wild and fierce and sharp as the lightning and just as reasonless."

Among our newer poets James Agee shows a decided Jeffers influence in his longer poem *Ann Garner*.

This narrative has symbolic significance, poetic strength and superb technique, but lacks that bold psycho-realistic depth which makes Jeffers stand out among American poets of our generation.

"Glamis hath murder'd sleep, and therefore Cawdor shall sleep no more," might be used as a motto for Jeffers's *Cawdor*. This poem was intended by the author to form the third, together with *Tamar* and *The Women at Point Sur,* of what might be called inspirations from classic drama. Yet he has used his material in an entirely original and characteristic way.

Cawdor is the story of an orphan girl who has escaped with her father the great forest fire of 1909 in California, marries the ranch owner, Cawdor, and falls in love with his son. The consummation of the whole poem is not love, but death. All the characters live inwardly for themselves, not outwardly or creatively. It is a study of pity born out of suffering and pain, of imprisonment of personality, and the struggle of the soul to free itself from this confinement. The freeing through death of the wounded eagle, the broken-winged "messenger of human love," symbolizes the ultimate victory of pity. Just as Ibsen uses the wild duck to signify the misery *motif*, so Jeffers employs the eagle. Cawdor at the end slashes out his own eyes. By losing his eyes, he begins to see and to desire something outside "the filthy nothing, the fouled and rotten faces of rich and successful men." For

Something had flown away, oh cage-hoarded desire,
Like a blade of a breaking wave reaped by the wind,
        or flame rising from fire, or cloud-coiling lightning
Suddenly unfurled in the cave of heaven: I that am
        stationed and cold at heart, incapable of burning,
My blood like standing sea-water lapped in a stone
        pool,
My desire to the rock, how can I speak of you?

The spirit of the eagle, with Jeffers's eyes, beholds the
world: man as a physical being becomes absurdly min-
ute and futile in comparison with universal forces and
the inexplicable mystery of life, as though the bird en-
visioned that "undiscovered country" of which Shakespeare speaks, revealing its dark secrets to us who "can
know the living world only symbolically." The eagle's
spirit, burning and soaring, sees

The shining ocean below lay on the shore
Like the great shield of the moon come down, rolling
        bright rim to rim with the earth.
Against it the multiform and many-canyoned coast
        range hills were gathered into one carven moun-
        tain, one modulated
Eagle's cry made stone, stopping the strength of the
        sea. The beaked and winged effluence
Felt the air foam under its throat and saw
The mountain sun-cup Tassajara, where fawns
Dance in the steam of the hot fountains at dawn,
Smoothed out, and the high strained ridges beyond
        Cachagua,
Where the rivers are born and the last condor is dead,

Flatten, and a hundred miles toward morning the
    Sierras
Dawn with their peaks of snow, and dwindle and
    smooth down
On the globed earth.

Of the two poems *Dear Judas* and *The Loving Shepherdess* Jeffers himself has written: "There is some relationship between the two poems . . . the shepherdess in one and Judas and Jesus in the other, each embodying different aspects of love; nearly pure, therefore undeluded, but quite inefficient in the first, pitying in the second, possessive in the third."

To readers of Rénan's sceptical *Life of Jesus*, Berguer's psychoanalytical biographical study, George Moore's imaginative picture of Jesus in *Brook Kerith,* or the historical textual study of John M. Robertson, *Jesus and Judas,* Jeffers's Jesus, too, will be a living image of the unorthodox, God-intoxicated Son of Man, determined to search till death for the dark, bottomless infinite abyss of life infused with a spirit of joy arising from the old self. Jesus says:

> Dear Judas, it is not God drives us.
> It is not shameful to be duped by God.
> I have known his glory in my life-time
> I have been his glory. I know
> Beyond illusion the enormous beauty of the torch in
>   which our agonies are all particles of fire.

Jeffers's Christ is at times possessed with an almost earthly lust for power, power to be alive:

> More tyrannous, more terrible, more true than Caesar
>   or any subduer of the earth before him has dared
>   to dream of
> In a dream . . .

Striving against this craving for power we have Judas, who perhaps has the source of his being in the poet's own hypersensitive nature. Jesus says to Judas:

> To other men I say be merciful, to you alone
> Be cruel. Life is not to be lived without some
>   balance . . .

Judas replies:

> Master, I am neither sick nor poor nor heavy with
>   sins,
> But I am in prison of my pity; the moaning of men
>   and beasts torments me; the pain is not my own
>   pain
> From which I come praying for deliverance.

Jesus asks:

>   Does it make you glad
> To see men joyful? To watch them feasting or laugh-
>   ing or fine with drunkenness?

Judas replies:

>   Master, I don't know why,
> But I am never joyful to see that. Certainly I'm not
>   grieved, but the others' joy is not mine,

Only their pain. My heart is lonely: I groan for their
  pain.

Jesus:

You have then only the night side of love,
Be with me, Judas, and I will teach you to love by day
  and by night.

Here we see Christ, the extrovert, versus Judas, the
introvert. What could the purely sensitive soul of Judas do but try to save his Master from the inevitable
results of his thirst for this all too worldly power, even
if he has to betray him in order to save him from unconsciously self-imposed destruction? "To let the people alone is the mercy: all stirring is death to them,"
pleads Judas. But Jesus ignores his plea and goes to his
doom in the outer world saying:

There is not one creature,
Neither yourself nor anyone, nor a
Fly nor flung stone, but does not exactly and fatally
  the thing
That it needs must; neither more nor less.
This is the root of forgiveness.
This is our secret, Judas.
For the people's hearts are not scrupulous like yours,
    and if they heard it they'd run on license and die
In the falling and splitting world, now that the sword
    and civilization and exile will break the sureties
And ungroove the lives . . . I bid you beware of the
    net, fishermen.
You see men walking and they seem to be free but
    look at the faces, they're caught . . .

"The great book which Jesus read and re-read was that of humanity," says Berguer in his book, *Some Aspects of the Life of Jesus*. In other words, Jesus was of the extrovert type—"one who turned toward the outward world, whose feelings expressed themselves entirely in external action," while Judas "thinks about what surrounds them, to reflect upon the external and internal events of their lives." According to St. Luke (XXII, 3-5) Satan entered into Judas while he sat among the other Disciples partaking of the Passover. What if we take this physically expressed fact and translate it into poetic truth, or that Goethean-Mephistophelian truth of the spirit, "which always wills the bad, but does the good?" Some writers maintain that Judas was enlightened by this Satanic or demonic spirit's voice, and that he acted in accordance with the dictates of this voice in order that mankind might be redeemed through the death of Christ. "It is a mistake to think of Judas as a demon without any element of goodness and grace. His repentance may be taken to imply that the 'traitor' had deceived himself by a false hope that, after all, his Master might pass through the midst of his enemies unscathed as he had done before on the brow of the mountain."

To appreciate fully the character of Clare Walker in *The Loving Shepherdess* we must recall St. John,

XXI:17: "He said unto him the third time: 'Simon, son of Jonas, lovest thou me?' Peter was grieved because he said unto him the third time, 'Lovest thou me?' And he said unto him, 'Thou knowest that I love thee.' Jesus saith unto him, 'Feed my sheep.' "

Clare Walker, the wanderer, represents the force of self-sacrifice striving against the brutal strength of reality. She might be called a symbol of Ghandi's passive resistance in action, poetically expressed. Love to her is a supreme duty, the spirit of Christ urging her always to give herself in all possible ways. It is a challenge to those who, with Nietzsche, accuse Christianity of softness and meanness. Clare Walker is possessed by the spirit of strength; she believes in a God who is human kindness. Homeless, destitute, heavy with child, she will not leave her sheep until death itself takes her from them or them from her. "I'm doing like most other people, take care of those that need me; and go on till I die." Such beings live in order that "the superior good may exist; the inferior good must be annihilated." Clare Walker belongs to "these little women that call out to humanity in the blackness of the night . . . they utter a cry of compassion, and they hold your hand in their emaciated hands. They understand only when you are unhappy; they can cry with you and console you—but they cannot laugh with you." What becomes of these when they leave us?—when their sheep are gone?

Clare had gone half a mile
And felt a grinding pain in her back, she clung to
    the fence
And saw the poplars planted along the road
Reach dreadfully away northward.
When the pain ended
She went on northwest; but after the second pain
She crept down to the river and hid her body
In a willow thicket. In the evening between the rapid
Summits of agony before exhaustion, she called
The sheep about her and perceived that none came.

"The pathos of this extraordinary story is overwhelming," writes Percy Hutchison in his sympathetic review of this poem. "If any but hardened reviewers can read it without tears, they do not perhaps deserve to read it."

In *The Loving Shepherdess* and to a lesser degree in *Cawdor,* Jeffers's spirit of tragedy has attained what Joseph Wood Krutch conceives as "essentially an expression, not of despair, but of triumph over despair and of confidence in the value of human life." In both *The Loving Shepherdess* and *Dear Judas* we have the tragic conception of what Krutch calls "a profession of faith, and a sort of religion; a way of looking at life by virtue of which it is robbed of its pain. The sturdy soul of the tragic author seizes upon suffering and uses it only as a means by which joy may be wrung out of existence."

In *The Humanist's Tragedy,* King Pentheus who had the temerity to oppose the introduction into Thebes of the frenzied worship of Dionysus, is mistaken by his own mother, a convert to the new faith, for a wild beast and torn to pieces. In this fragment suggested by Euripides's *Bacchae* Jeffers inveighs against the world-old tendency of nations and their rulers to resist the new and unfamiliar, a characteristic which, in the poet's opinion, has betrayed humanity as bitterly as Jacob's mess of pottage betrayed Esau. The description of the god, Dionysus, passing through his crowd of followers "like a tall ship breasting through water" is one of the most superb similes in modern poetry.

In *Thurso's Landing,* by means of Reave's terrible accident and death, Jeffers not only proclaims his own personal dislike for modern civilization, and man's futile attempts to conquer nature, but he also symbolizes the tragedy of the modern era. Reading this poem brings to mind a passage from D. H. Lawrence: "What really torments civilized people is that they are full of feelings they know nothing about; they can't realize them, they can't live them. And so they are tortured. It is like having energy you can't use. It destroys you."

Jeffers's attitude toward the machine age is clearly indicated in the following passage:

> the hopeless prostration of the earth
> Under men's hands and their minds,
> The beautiful places killed like rabbits to make a city,
> The spreading fungus, the slime—threads

And spores: my own coast's obscene future.
I remember the farther
Future, and the last man dying
Without succession under confident eyes of the stars.
It was only a moment's accident,
The race that plagued us; the world resumes the old
     lonely, immortal
Splendor; from here I can even
Perceive that the snuffed candle had something . . .
     a fantastic virtue,
A faint and unshapely pathos . . .

The above as well as many forceful passages in *Thurso's Landing* itself—as for instance "I wish they'd let the poor old road be. I don't like improvements— they bring in the world; we're well without it"—give the underlying *motif* of the poem.

By this time we understand the poet himself as well as the embodiments of his poetic tendency. He analyses and interprets his characters by his "poetic omniscience"; in other words, he enters into the characters, their hidden motives, their tragic backgrounds and natures. According to Jeffers, men are born rhythm-breakers on the wheel called life, therefore they create tragic situations within and without themselves. The poet's imagery and poetic thoughts are what William James calls "projected outwards." To the unimaginative reader or reviewer they might seem lacking in "character of objective reality." Some of Jeffers's critics do not realize that so-called poetic virility is measured entirely by the poet's power to reproduce out of realistic wholes only the things that are most certain and sympathetic to his own psyche. Ibsen's phrase that the writing of poetry is "to hold Doomsday over ones-self" could be applied to any creator of original art.

In *Thurso's Landing* it is clear that Jeffers possesses, as does Thomas Hardy, a marked sensitiveness to local scenes and atmospheres. In the work of both poets we find the protagonists usually lonely, isolated, sometimes childless individuals, for whom family ties seem to count little.

Let us take at random some of Jeffers's lines as he skillfully and with unusual facility for the use—and omission—of words, paints pictures for the reader:

> The group dissolved apart, having made for a moment its unconscious beauty
> In the vast landscape above the ocean in the colored evening; the naked bodies of the young bathers
> Polished with light, against the brown and blue denim core of the rest; and the ponies, one brown, one piebald,
> Compacted into the group, the Spanish-Indian horseman dark bronze above them, under red
> Heavens leaning to the lonely mountain.

Or this:

> In the moonlight two hours before Sunday dawn
> Rick Armstrong went on foot over the hill
> Toward the farmhouse in the deep gorge, where it was dark
> And he smelled the stream.

And the falling of the great tree which caused the accident:

> But the others watched . . . the high oak-tree
> Rush down the hill, the arched balks and crooked
>   thighs
> Of root in the scant soil on the near rock
> Channelled with dry-rot, proving less masterful
> Than one inch twist of hemp; so avalanche-like
> The whole tree went down to the gorge, from its great
>   yellow furrow on the face of the hill
> A long track of dust blew east, above and below
> The racing clouds.

How like Hardy in power of purely aesthetic observation and dramatic presentation! Here we see the passionate self desiring to enlarge itself by the universal not-self. A British critic has very cleverly said: "If the United States had gone the way of Whitman and Emily Dickinson, it might have become one hundred percent human instead of one hundred percent American." This is the tragedy of *Thurso's Landing.*

A shorter poem in the same volume, *Margrave,* is a miniature of Dostoievsky's *Crime and Punishment.* In this the murderer excuses his crime in the name of science and to help humanity against the *malaise* which is destroying western civilization.

This volume of Jeffers's poems ends

> On a little stone-girdled platform
> Over the earth and the ocean
> I seem to have stood a long time and watched the
>   stars pass.
> They also shall perish, I believe.
> Here today, gone tomorrow, desperate wee galaxies
> Scattering themselves and shining their substance away
> Like a passionate thought. It is very well ordered.

The hawk is to the Egyptians the symbol of the soul, and it is in this sense that Jeffers employs it as a symbol in his poetry. In the Egyptian language *bai* means the soul, *eth* the heart; the combination of the two, *baieth,* is the word for hawk. In *Give Your Heart to the Hawks* we hear the primitive music, the long, wild, profound complaint which echo repeats in distant sobs, inspiring sombre thoughts and shades of melancholy as from the heart of Shelley's Prometheus. Jeffers writes:

> The poet, who wishes not to play games with words,
> His affair being to awake dangerous images
> And call the hawks—they all feed the future, they
>   serve God,
> Who is very beautiful, but hardly a friend of hu-
>   manity.

Give Your Heart to the Hawks opens with the emblem of sexual life, passion and vitality, the serpent, and ends on "a dizzy and lonely place on a height," where men feel they "have to peel off some of humanness or it will be hard to live." Most of the action transpires in the dark of the moon. According to the Upanishads, this is a period of evolution, the animal-man is passing through matter to reach the sun, or higher self. Instinctive acts and primitive sexual passion are as closely interwoven into the action of this poem as of the others we have discussed. At times it seems as though Jeffers's own consciousness is the only witness of the tragic physical and psychological conflicts of his characters. In this, his latest volume, as in his earlier, Jeffers is looking forward beyond the present age of transition and negation into an unborn future. Like some of Dostoievsky's works, Flaubert's *La Legende de Saint-Julien l'Hospitalier,* Emily Brontë's *Wuthering Heights,* and Jack Lindsay's *The Lady and the Mute,* this is the tragedy of a great hater, a self-hater, to whom hate becomes a mania. It is hatred such as Ortega y Gasset describes, hatred which means extermination and virtual murder. "It is not murder which is accomplished with one stroke; it means to murder incessantly and to obliterate the hated object from the world." In Jeffers's poem the hated object is Lance himself, after he has killed his brother "for nothing." In order to punish himself, his own humanity, Lance becomes one with nature and imitates her law. He kills and kills and kills, and never tires of killing until he learns the terrible lesson man is so slow in learning—that nature can

never be conquered; only through conforming to her
can man be

> Able to live, in spite of pain and that horror and the
>   dear blood on your hands, and your father's God,
> To be able to go on in pure silence
> In your own power, not panting for people's judg-
>   ment, nor the pitiful consolation of punishing
>   yourself
> Because an old man filled you with dreams of sin
> When you were little: you are not one of the sparrows,
>   you are not a flock-bird; but alone in your nature,
> Separate as a gray hawk.

In this poem Jeffers conceives humanity as having
reached the stage of adolescence; influences of childhood and of school days are slowly and painfully being
discarded. A new future is being prepared for. Lance
is a symbol of natural man crushed by human systems
into extreme multiplicity. He is almost himself, yet is
forced to live beyond himself because he harbors an
inner tragedy which hardens his spirit to the limit of
its endurance, whipping up all the primitive instincts
for destroying life—destroying himself. There is the
breaking away from religious orthodoxy represented
by old Fraser, and an acceptance of a personal epi-
curianism in Lance—an invitation to create for ourselves a revaluation of old standards, to create ideal
values "past the narrow of common faithfulness" embodied in Fayne who goes beyond mere hedonism.
She bears the seeds of a new race within her:

"Look, dear,
    How clear the quivering waters and white of dawn fill
        the whole world; they seem to wash the whole
        mountain
    All gently and white, and over the sea, purifying
        everything. If I were less tired
    I could be full of joy." She pressed her hands to her
        throat and swallowed and said, "Where you and I
    Have come to, is a dizzy and lonely place on a height;
        we have to peel off
    Some humanness here or it will be hard to live.
    If you could think that all human feelings, repentance
    And blood-thirst too, are not very important in so vast
        a world; nor anyone's life;
    Nor love either, the unlucky angel
    That has led me so far: we'll go on, we'll not fail.
        All over the mountain
    The eagles and little falcons and all the bright cold
        hawks—you've made friends with them now—
        are widening
    Their wings to wash them in the cool clearness, and
        over the precipices launching their bodies like
        ships
    On the high waves of dawn. For us too
    Dawn brings us wandering; and any ghost or memory·
        that wants to follow us will be sore in the feet
    Before the day's end. We're going until the world
        changes, you and I like the young hawks
    Going hunting; we'll take the world by the throat
        and make him give us
    What we desire."

The tragedy ends on a note of hope with Fayne
climbing up, "rock to rock, bush to bush," toward the

sun. She is heavy with child; "this child in my body will change the world." The child conceived by *homo praeteritus* will be the child of *homo futurus:*

> Beautiful blossoms of battle again and forever un-
> folding
> Star of the earth, but we dropped petals of one
> Shall endure peace, not even to behold them again nor
> to hear them,
> In the quiet places, in enormous neutrality,
> Oh perfectly beautiful, pain is brief, endure to be
> sacrificed,
> This great age falls like water and a new
> Age is at birth, but without your pain it could never
> be beautiful.

Most of the types in Jeffers's long narrative poems are the same we find in Hardy's novels, types combining "modern nerves with primitive emotions."

In Melville, Conrad, Morley Roberts, D. H. Lawrence, J. C. Powys, Sean O'Faolain, and Rhys Davies we meet the same types. They are inheritors of sensual visions, earthly dreams and tragic destinies in spite of civilization, education and social causes.

They are seekers after a lost God in the turmoil of modernity. They have a passion for the actual, yet in their inmost being they apprehend forces which are at war with the actualities of their age. They are mostly lonely types we meet in these authors' works, they prefer to feel that "in loneliness a human being feels himself backward, down the long series of his avatars, into the earlier planetary life of animals, birds, and reptiles, and even into the cosmogonic life of rocks and stones."

Melville's gigantic white whale, the evil force in the universe, haunts them "down the labyrinthine ways" and they in return are hunting it "down the arches" of their years. Many readers of D. H. Lawrence and no doubt of Jeffers's narrative poems object to the sex abnormalities there. They are there, but we must see them with Freud, and if we "fail to understand these abnormal manifestations of sexuality and are unable to relate them to normal sexual life, then we cannot understand normal sexuality. It is, in short, our unavoidable task to account theoretically for all the potentialities of the perversions we have gone over and to explain their relation to the so-called normal sexuality."

The second long poem in the volume is called *Resurrection*. It is the story of a dead lover's return to life to claim his beloved now wedded to another man. The poem concludes with the union of Hildis, the wife, and Carson, the resurrected lover. As a climax to the action Jeffers gives us a beautiful love poem of deep feeling:

> They went out together,
> And down the gross darkness of the night mountain.
> They were rather like one star than two people,
> for that night at least,
> So love had joined them to burn a moment for each
> other, no other star was needed in all the black
> world.

But love or hatred
Or good or evil are hardly
A hair's weight here in the balance.
One being risen from the dead,
The irrational mind revives,
All things are possible again.

The third poem, *At the Fall of an Age,* is Jeffers's hymn to imaginative beauty, with Helen of Troy as the symbol of what Keats calls "truth and beauty," or reality and beauty. We recall Plato's *Symposium:* "The true order of going or being led by another to the things of love is to use beauties of the earth as steps along which he mounts upward for the sake of that beauty." The poem ends with a lyrical neo-classical coda which conveys the "blessing of a new age at birth with the beauty of her body"—the body of Helen, "the one lonely beauty left in the world, as lonely as the last eagle":

Wild swan, splendid-bodied,
Silent at last, silent and proud, fly up the dark.
Clash bronze, beat shields, beauty is new-born.
It is not to be whispered in Argos that Helen died like
    a woman,
Nor told in Laconia that sickness killed her.
Strike swords, blade on blade, the daughter of God
Hangs like a lamp, high in the dark, quivering and
    white.
The breasts are thrust forward, and the head bows, the
    fleece of gold

Shakes on the straining shoulders, writhes to the long
thighs.
When God looked down from heaven the mound in
the Troad
Swarmed like an ant-hill, the spears from the dark
barrow . . .
Look under the torches.
No Dorians are we; they planted strange seed in Asia
who buried Achilles,
Power to pierce death, helmeted heads cracking the
grass-roots,
Power to be born again.
Come down and behold us Oh King of heaven and
Oh hawks of Caucasus
Come down and behold us,
You African lions in the tawny wilderness roar in the
storm,
For our master is joined with the beauty he remem-
bered in death, with the splendor of the earth . . .

The above is Jeffers's version of Thoreau's saying:
"I have been as sincere a worshipper of Aurora as the
Greeks . . . Morning brings back the heroic age."
With *Solstice and other Poems* we must place our-
selves between truths of the past and truths of the
present in order to realise that our

angry choices and hopes and terrors are in vain,
But life and death not in vain; and the world is like
a flight of swans.

It is natural that at this time of the Italo-Ethiopian
conflict, Nazi anti-Semitic, anti-humanistic indulgence

upon brute instinct, we are bound to stop here and there while reading Jeffers's latest poems, realising that we are living within the shadow of another world-war. Jeffers often confuses us. And some of the reviewers and critics, especially of this last volume, seem to have misunderstood his intent as much as Swinburne after reading *Leaves of Grass* for the first time: "Mr. Whitman's Eve is a drunken apple-woman, indecently sprawling in the slush and garbage of the gutter amid the rotten refuse of overturned fruit-stall; but Mr. Whitman's Venus is a Hottentot wench under the influence of cantharides and adulterated rum."

The first poem, or dramatic epos, *At the Birth of an Age,* deals with the devastating effects of invasion, such as swept over Europe in the fifth century, headed by the blond beast Attila, whom the dark ages named "Flagellum Dei." Not only the opening poem, but the whole volume of Solstice, is filled with terror and gloom of the Eddic 'ragna rok'; the fall of the house of the one-eyed Odin or Wodan whose wish-maidens, the valkyries, weep and wail while riding through this gloom on swift horses of the Apocalypse, recalling the chaotic valkyrie-ride music of Wagner.

"Over the earth are mighty battles. Brothers will slay each other for greeds sake; none spares father or mother in murder and incest," we read in one of the Eddic poems, which is the substance of what Jeffers has to say about our generation. Great are our attainments in our present so called civilization in science, in physics, in mechanics, economics, politics; and yet according to Jeffers, Robert Briffault and Bertrand Russell we are far from being civilized, but rather on the eve of a total collapse:

> I am not well civilized, really alien here; trust me not
> I can understand the guns and the air-planes,
> The other conveniences leave me cold

writes Jeffers.

It is in these lines that some Marxian-economist critics have found in Jeffers "a good Fascist propagandist." To put Jeffers's political views in concrete form let us quote from the December 1934 issue of *New Verse* which published answers from many modern poets to their enquiry which included six questions.

To the fifth question: "Do you stand with any political or politico-economy party or creed?" Jeffers answered "No."

Some of us might regret that Jeffers, like many poets, has not concerned himself with politics; not perhaps the politics of our day, but those of Eternity. For the genuine poet, in Blake's words, is "always above the ages." Jeffers, with Dante, Dostoievsky and Baudelaire, is not for immature minds who

> live insanely and desire
> with their tongues, progress, with their eyes pleasure.

Jeffers should be read only by minds spiritually awakened not by formulated theories, but by a clear vision of evil, or the Greek γνῶϛις; immediate vision of truth. As T. S. Eliot remarks, "Most people are only very little alive; and to awaken them to the spiritual is a very great responsibility; it is only when they are so awakened that they are capable of Good, but at the same time they become first capable of Evil."

No doubt Lucretius by *"terrorem animi"* meant the soul's tragic experience of evil in order to understand the nefarious savagery of the uncivilized, as well as the over-civilized, in a transitory state of social, as well as political progress.

Jeffers is, in Dryden's words, "The very Janus of poets; he wears almost everywhere two faces; and you have scarce begun to admire the one, ere you despise the other."

The Marxian critics err in translating works of art into terms of utilitarian or materialistic world-power, everything must fit Lenin's prescription: "Literature must become part of the general proletariat movement."

Jeffers, even when he tries to embody politico-social evils with all the precision of a very objective analysis, still maintains them to be the expression, not of realistic evils, but of directly experienced ideas of evil. The poet's experience is not reality, but "a reconciliation of truth with reality in thought."

In Jeffers evil becomes a direct antithesis to the Manichaen dualistic principle; the positive principle in collective humanity is evil; the negative being good. "The

problem of suffering and evil is always the greatest
enigma of being, after the existence of being itself," reflects Amiel in his meditations on evil.

Jeffers is against what we moderns term the bourgeois, perpetually blind flowing of happiness and empty
physical desires of the man in the street. These pleasures "leave him cold."

To Jeffers many of our civilized useful arts are tools
of tragic misapplication. "The guns and the air-planes"
are useful tools for blind Caesars as much as the new
economics of the new abundance are traps to catch the
unthinking masses in democratic happiness, material
prosperity and power of technicalized savagery—the
State.

Such bourgeois happiness as for instance Gilbert
Murray advocates: "We can only conquer Bolshevism
by making the mass of men happier than the Bolshe-
viks can make them" is to Jeffers worshipping the
"sacred rich" whom Dr. Carrel calls "the élite" of democracy.

The Marxian theorists, who seek in our poets political
or social propaganda as they happen to embrace it for
the moment, should remember that to every poet the
strength of individualism is more important than any
collectivist propaganda. To the poet, consciousness, and
not usefulness, is his question as a will to power.

We all know that communism and fascism limit individual liberty. For Jeffers there is "a great wisdom in
pain hidden from the happy" robot-like masses, made

happy by the bourgeois standards which the Russians imitate:

> Men suffer want and become
> Curiously ignoble; as prosperity
> Made them curiously vile.

The Marxian theorists would do better by placing Jeffers with Bertrand Russell between the two struggling camps of world-power: "Fascists and Communists" writes Russell "having in their minds a picture of society as a whole distort individuals to make them fit into a pattern: those who cannot be adequately distorted are killed or placed in concentration camps."

Many of our young Marxian critics seem to pursue their propaganda in accordance with what they hear rather than with what they actually believe, therefore their "shallow spirit of judgment." They do not seem to realise that poetry, like all other arts, aims at presenting to the reader's mind the completeness of a creative act as the poet or artist has conceived it in his intellectual as well as imaginative experience. And this experience comprises more than readings of Marx, Engels or Lenin. It is more than theoretic knowledge of economics, sociology and politics; for all the sufferings and the cruelties humanity endures in Jeffers work are rooted in the poet's own intellectual and moral agony: for he has "chosen Being: therefore wounds, bonds, limits and pain! the crowded mind and the anguished nerves, experience and ecstasy." Jeffers sees with Dante

the mystery of life from its blindest, bleakest and cruel-
lest side:

> Praise life, it deserves praise, but the praise of life
> That forgets the pain is a pebble
> Rattled in a dry gourd.

At the Birth of an Age ends with Prometheus, Jeffers's eagle-Christ, crying crucified upon the bleeding
body of this earth and hearing humanity's endless cries:

> How they cry to me! but they are I: let them ask
>   themselves.
> I am they, and there is nothing beside.
> I am alone and time passes, time also is in me, the long
> Beat of this unquiet heart, the quick drip of this
>   blood, the whirl and returning waves of these
>   stars,
> The course of this thought . . .
>
> *   *   *   *
>
> I am the nerve, I am the agony,
> I am endurance. I torture myself
> To discover myself . . .
>
> *   *   *   *
>
> Discovery is deep and endless,
> Each moment of being is new; therefore I still refrain
>   my burning thirst from the crystal-black
> Water of an end.

The dramatic epos written from the "summit of a
wave of this age" ends with

> Mysticism of stone which failure cannot cast down
> Nor success make proud.

Considered as a work of perfected art in comparison
with *The Tower Beyond Tragedy,* this poem bears the
mark of incompleteness—yet it has a

> Power to make
> Our noisy years seem moments in the being
> Of the eternal silence.

With *Solstice,* the second longest poem in this volume, we are back on familiar ground, the coast of California "crying out for tragedy."

To understand Jeffers's version of the Medea complex
we would do well to reread Aristotle's conception of
tragedy in relation to poetics, though this cannot be
applied in its entirety to Jeffers's theme.

The story is concise, vivid and arresting, but its motive force is not that of penetrating pity as in *The Loving Shepherdess,* and the emotions it arouses are not
purged by pity, but a blind brutal terror of the
"ἀναγνώριδις," or the stark realisation of a tragic error.

Madrone Bothwell,

> a fierce unsubdued core
> That lives in the high rock in the heart of the con-
>   tinent, affronting the bounties of civilization and
>   Christ,
> Troublesome, contemptuous, archaic, with thunder-
>   storm hair and snowlike eyes, waiting . . .

is less Euripedes's Medea than Guthrum from the
Greenland ballad of Atlamol who:

bitterly planned . . . and
Buthli's race threatened,
And terrible vengeance on her husband would take.

We must approach and read *Solstice* with Jeffers's personal philosophy in mind; Madrone Bothwell acts in accordance with that particular Jeffers revolt against the mechanical order of things.

Madrone's will, "free will" if we wish to call it, breaks through social systems and conventions. Her will which dates from prehistoric times cannot see her children, the next generation, in the robot-like existence of a totalitarian State. Madrone's will could be called the will of nature revolting under the yoke of man's self-imposed tyranny. We also feel that her sexual love, or loves, have been founded upon spiritual hate as Yeats would say.

Of course Madrone, or nature, cannot stop industrialization of the world, but she resolves to stop her children from becoming a future part in our restless de-humanization of humanity. She cannot see them

> grow up and be sold for toys.
> . . . having no center
> But in the eyes and mouths that surround them,
>
> Having no function but to serve and support civilization, the enemy of man

Madrone acts as if under the barbarous, overmastering impulse of some dictatorial violence; rather death for her children than see them debauched by modern Attilas whose dictums might be the cause of her crime. We must remember that Madrone's "emotions have little value in themselves," as Dr. George E. Moore states in his *Principia Ethics:* "The state of mind in which they exist may have its value greatly heightened, or may entirely lose it and become positively evil in a great degree, according as the cognition accompanying the emotions are appropriate or inappropriate; so the appreciation of these emotions, though it may have some value in itself, may yet form a part of a whole which has greater value or no value at all according as it is or is not accompanied by a perception of the appropriateness of the emotions to their objects." In other words, Madrone is still the free-willed animal not yet properly adapted to such inhuman slogans:—

"I absolutely disbelieve in perpetual peace which is detrimental to the fundamental virtues of man. War is to man what maternity is to woman." So Mussolini repeatedly declares. Hitler says: "In the brains of the smallest child should be implanted this ardent appeal, 'Almighty God, bless our arms,' " and Lenin says: "It doesn't matter a jot if three-fourths of mankind perish; the only thing that matters is that, in the end, the remaining fourth should become Communist."

In all Jeffers's tragic conflicts we must, as Hegel points out, "place on one side the false notion of guilt or innocence." The heroes of Jeffers's tragedies "are quite as much under the one category as the other . . .

"They act in accordance with a specific character, a

specific pathos, for the simple reason that they are this character, this pathos . . . They are simply themselves, and never anything else, and their greatness or weakness consists in that fact."

We might end *Solstice*, after Madrone has laid the slain children "to bed in the wet earth," with the words from a shorter poem in the same volume:

> now you are free, even to become human
> But born of the rock and the air, not woman

Thus according to Jeffers mystical *Weltauschauung* the children have become human through the inhuman outer world and will not be wasted "inward upon humanity."

And so we leave the dark inner world of Jeffers's tragedies, the world as Zola pictured it—an overcrowded railroad train, with bloodstained and mean power-drunk soldiers dashing through the dark night to some disaster.

PART V

ATTITUDE TOWARD POETRY, CIVILIZATION AND NATURE

You never enjoy the world aright till you
so love the beauty of enjoying it that you
are covetous and earnest to persuade others
to enjoy it. And so perfectly hate the abom-
inable corruption of men in despising it that
you would rather suffer the flames of hell
than willingly be guilty of their error.

Traherne

ATTITUDE TOWARD POETRY, CIVILIZATION AND NATURE

JEFFERS has been accused, as Lucretius was, of preaching the gospel of human annihilation, a *mors immortalis, mors aeterna.* The Epicurean two-fold *securitas,* the everlasting human yearning for freedom from distress, for the sacred security of eternal nothingness, is "as old and new at once as nature's self." According to Lucretius, the world is a dead machine. He, too, lived in an age when the dread of individuality, which has always animated the lives of the masses, was expressed by deadly violence on the part of the people as a whole. The first necessity of the Roman state of his day was that of our communistic Russia—to rid the country of political tyrants. It was only natural that Lucretius should escape from the restlessness of his time by seeking refuge in nature. The East Indian ideal of resignation pervades *De Rerum Natura,* that epic of redemption. Lucretius yearned for nature as a man yearns to escape from something terribly infectious—over-civilization.

Johan Huizinga's reference to conditions in the Middle Ages might well be applied to our present state: "Always and everywhere in the literature of the age we find a confessed pessimism. As soon as the soul of these

147

men has passed from childlike mirth and unreasoning enjoyment to reflection, deep dejection about all earth- ly misery takes place and they see only the woe of life. Still this very pessimism is the ground whence their souls will soar up to the aspiration of a life of beauty and security. For at all times the vision of a sublime life has haunted the souls of poets, and the gloomier the present is, the more strongly this aspira- tion will make itself felt. Strongest and most lasting of all is the illusion of a return to nature and its innocent charms by an imitation of the shepherd life. Since Theocritus it has never lost its hold upon civilized society."

It seems that every poet ponders upon the emptiness of his own epoch. Jeffers believes, not in a progress and adjustment made possible by a scientific control of life, but rather in a redeeming change in the individual himself, in his inner life, his values, his desires—the Nietzschean will to spiritual power—a consciousness peculiar to an age on its death-bed. "Is not the night becoming darker and darker? Must we not light our lanterns at noon? Do you not already hear the noise of the grave-diggers who are burying God? God is dead! God will remain dead! And we have killed God. How shall we be consoled for this, we murderers of murderers?"—this from *The Joyful Wisdom,* one of Nietzsche's utterances in the style of the *Psalms* and *Proverbs.*

Jeffers's attitude toward his own poetry is expressed in the following lines from his poem, *Point Joe:*

> Permanent things are what is needful in a poem, things temporarily
> Of great dimension, things constantly renewed or always present:
> Grass that is made earth each year equals the mountains in her past and future:
> Fashionable and momentary things we need not see nor speak of.

As antithesis to the above we place the last lines from MacLeish's *Sentiments for a Dedication:*—

> I speak to those of my own time
> To none other
> I say Remember me Remember this one rhyme
> I say Remember me among you in that land my brothers
> O living men Remember me Receive me among you.

We feel that MacLeish has lost the essential poetic heritage Shelley speaks of in his preface to *The Revolt of Islam:*—

"I have considered poetry in its most comprehensive sense and have read the poets and the historians and the metaphysicians whose writings have been accessible to me, and have looked upon the beautiful and majestic scenery of the earth as common source of those elements which it is the province of the poet to embody and combine."

"The beautiful and majestic scenery of the earth" dominates Jeffers's poetry, while MacLeish remains a chanter of the "fashionable and momentary things."

In order to emphasize the correlation between Shelley and Jeffers in combining in their poetry subjective idealism and objective realism we may quote from the anthropologic philosophy of Max Scheler, reflecting a similar view:—

"He whose roots are deepest in the dark depth of the earth and Nature—that 'natura naturans' which primally and eternally brings forth the tangible forms of Nature, the 'natura Naturata'—and he who at the same time as Person towers highest in his spiritual self-consciousness, in the bright world of Ideas, he it is who draws nearer to the idea of the Whole-man and, in a certain sense, to the idea of the Eternal Substance itself, that Substance which has its Being in the steadily becoming interpenetration of Spirit and Urge."

Even the most mechanistic-minded among us feel unconsciously this call to something beyond a materialistic universe, a call which we might term the "will to nature," where no conscious motive is present. In a longer poem called *The Artist,* Jeffers's poetic urge is felt "leading to some unbearable consummation of the ecstasy":

"Sympathy? Praise? I have never desired them and
      also I have never deserved them. I will not show
      you
More than the spalls you saw by accident.

What I see is the enormous beauty of things, but what
    I attempt
Is nothing to that. I am helpless toward that.
It is only the form in stone, the mould of some ideal
    humanity that might be worthy to be
Under the lightning. Animalcules that God (if he
    were given to laughter) might omit to laugh at.

"Those children of my hands are tortured because they
    feel the storm of the outer magnificence.
They are giants in agony. They have seen from my
    eyes
The man-destroying beauty of the dawns over their
    notch yonder, and all the obliterating stars.
But in their eyes they have peace. I have lived a little
    and I think
Peace marrying pain alone can breed that excellence
    in the luckless race, might make it decent
To exist at all on the star-lit stone breast."

The imagination as well as the eye is always at work in Jeffers's poetry. He gives us nature naked, heightened, shining as though newly created. His attitude toward poetry is further shown in *Soliloquy:*

August and laurelled have been content to speak for
    an age, and the ages that follow
Respect them for that pious fidelity;
But you have disfeatured time for timelessness.
They had heroes for companions, beautiful youths to
    dream of, rose-marble-fingered
Women shed light down the great lines;
But you have invoked the slime in the skull,

The lymph in the vessels. They have shown men Gods
  like racial dreams, the woman's desire,
The man's fear, the hawk-faced prophet's; but nothing
Human seems happy at the feet of yours.
Therefore though not forgotten, not loved, in gray old
  years in the evening leaning
Over the gray stones of the tower-top,
You shall be called heartless and blind;
And watch new time answer old thought, not a face
  strange nor a pain astonishing;
But you living be laired in rock
That sheds pleasure and pain like hail-stones.

And in the following:

If one should tell them what's clearly seen
They'd not understand; if they understood they would
  not believe;
If they understood and believed they'd say,
"Hater of men, annihilating with a sterile enormous
Splendor our lives: where are our lives?"
A little chilled perhaps, but not hurt. But it's quite
  true
The invulnerable love is not bought for nothing.
It is better no doubt to give crumbs than the loaf;
  make fables again,
Tell people not to fear death, toughen
Their bones if possible with bitter fables not to fear
  life.
—And one's own, not to have pity too much;
For it seems compassion sticks longer than the other
  colors, in this bleaching cloth.

In this we see Jeffers's own attitude toward "the public," as indifferent as that of Keats: "I have not the

slightest feel of humanity toward the public or to anything in existence but the Eternal Being, the Principle
of Beauty, and the memory of great men."

At the close of *Continent's End* we find how and
where the poet learned his rhythm, the irregular
rhythms of ordinary speech, at times breaking into
hexameters of the sixteenth century adopted by English poets from Greek and Latin verse:

> Mother, though my song's measure is like your surf-
>   beats' ancient rhythm I never learned it of you.
> Before there was any water there were tides of fire;
>   both our tones flow from the older fountain.

This "older fountain" Jeffers calls

> the single-eyed glare of the sun
> Flying southwest to the mountain . . .

In one of his poems Jeffers affirms:—

> It is bitter earnestness
> That makes beauty.

Besides his poetry we find this "bitter earnestness"
as the governing principle in such modern works of
permanent value as Proust's timeless, subjective novel,
Van Gogh's paintings, Scriabine's music, and in the outstanding sculptures of Jacob Epstein.

We discover in these works a power that germinates,
or rather harmonizes the juxtaposed, psychopathic
mind-forces termed the "protopathic" and the "epi-
critic"—the artist's capacity to express the "destroyer,"

the negative, and the "preserver," the positive forces with which the soul of man is doomed to struggle in the darkest depths of its humanity.

"It is not usually our ideas that make us optimists or pessimists," writes Unamuno. "But it is an optimism or a pessimism of physiological or perhaps pathological origin, as much the one as the other, that makes our ideas and these ideas into poetry." The logical and technical qualities of the poet's verse are subordinated to his creative vision. Thus we get in Jeffers's poetry, not a labored product, but a free activity—an utterance flowing direct from his own individual, personal experiences, as with Whitman, Blake and Wordsworth. The last characterizes thus the poetic mind: "The poet is chiefly distinguished from other men by a greater promptness to think and feel without immediate external excitement, and a greater power in expressing such thoughts and feelings as are produced in him in that manner." Krutch describes the poetic mind as "a tensely vigorous activity in which, for once, intelligence and knowledge seem, for the moment at least, reconciled with aspiration." Jeffers's nature poetry, like Milton's, "hath terror in it." Sometimes Wordsworth also reminds us of him:

> Humanity divorced,
> Humanity splitting the race of man
> In twain, yet leaving the same outward form
> Distress the mind ensued upon the sight,
> The ardent meditation . . .

And this passage also from Wordsworth:

> Alone upon the rock—oh, then the calm
> And dead still water lay upon my mind,
> Even with a weight of pleasure, and the sky,
> Never before so beautiful, sunk down
> Into my heart.

Nature in Wordsworth as in Jeffers becomes a feeling, a vision, an aspiration, not possessing thought nor logicalness, yet with a consciousness of man's being—a nature such as the pre-Socratic philosophers postulated —a universal entity with unchanging, unchartered laws of its own. In Chinese philosophy this conception is called "universism," and has its origin in both worship of nature and of ancestors (the dead).

Gerard Manley Hopkins was in the habit of calling this entity "inscape" into nature in order to reach God: "All the world is full of inscape and chance left free to act falls into an order as well as purpose."

This "inscape" into the external or unhuman world in order to project its significance Jeffers shows most clearly in a shorter poem *Love the Wild Swan:*

> I hate my verses, every line, every word,
> Oh pale and brittle pencils ever to try
> One grass-blade's curve, or the throat of one bird
> That clings to twig, ruffled against white sky.
> Oh cracked and twilight mirrors ever to catch
> One color, one glinting flash, of the splendor of things.
> Unlucky hunter, Oh bullets of wax,

The lion beauty, the wild-swan wings, the storm of
    the wings.
—This wild swan of a world is no hunter's game.
Better bullets than yours would miss the white breast,
Better mirrors than yours would crack in the flame.
Does it matter whether you hate your . . . self? At
    least
Love your eyes that can see, your mind that can
Hear the music, the thunder of the wings. Love the
    wild swan.

With Jeffers as with many of the eighteenth century poets, we live today in or with nature over the yesterdays of our childhood. We feel joy in knowing that there is something endurable, permanent; something that has not slipped away from us since the beginning of the earth. Jeffers's nature poetry is of earth and man. He has faith, not in man nor in his so-called progress, but in the earth-strong, eternal interchange of birth and death. Nature to him is remorseless theophany:

The old voice of the ocean, the bird-clatter of little
    rivers,
(Winter has given them gold for silver
To stain their water and bladed green for brown to
    line their banks)
From different throats in tune one language.
So I believe if we were strong enough to listen without
Divisions of desire and terror
To the storm of the sick nations, the rage of the
    hunger-smitten cities,

> Those voices also would be found clean as a child's;
>   or like some girl's breathing who dances alone
> By the ocean shore dreaming of lovers.

This is the kingdom of the nymphs who dwell by the sea which is equally divine with the earth. How tremendous is this great picture of night:

> Over the dark mountains, over the dark pinewood,
> Down the long dark valley along the shrunken river,
> Returns the splendor without rays, the shining of
>   shadow,
> Peace-bringer, the matrix of all shining and quieter
>   of shining.
> Where the shore widens on the bay she opens dark
>   wings
> And the ocean accepts her glory.
> O soul worshipful of her,
> You like the ocean have grave depths where she dwells
>   always.
> And the film of waves above that takes the sun takes
>   also
> Her, with more love. The sun-lovers have a blond
>   favorite,
> Hot labor, lust and delight and the other blemishes.
> Quietness
> Flows from her deepest fountain; and he will die;
>   and she is immortal.

Jeffers's is not a romanticized naturalism: He realizes dualism in nature as well as in man. Spiritually, he worships nature as the mother-image. The psycholo-

gists call this phenomenon *Ubertragung*—"the crossing" of the bridge to a new adaptation in life. The re-
pellent side of nature is seen in the following lines from
Tamar:

> the intolerably masculine sun hatefullest of all.
>   The heat of the season
> Multiplied centipedes, the black worms that breed
>   under loose rock, they call them thousand leggers,
> They invaded the house, their phalloid bodies crack-
>   ing underfoot with a bad odor, and dropped
> Ceiling to pillow at night, a vile plague though not
>   poisonous. Also the sweet and female sea
> Was weak with calm, one heard too clearly a mount-
>   ing cormorant's wing-claps half a mile off shore.

"New thoughts, however deep, are not the staple of
poetry," Wordsworth tells us, "but old thoughts presented with immortal freshness and a kind of inspired
felicity of diction." How well the following passages
from *Roan Stallion* illustrate this:

> after the leopard-footed evening
> Had glided oceanward, California turned the lamp to
>   its least flame and glided from the house.
> She moved sighing, like a loose fire, backward and for-
>   ward on the smooth ground by the door.
> She heard the night wind that draws down the valley
>   like the draught in a flue under clear weather
> Whisper and toss in the tall redwoods; she heard the
>   tinkle of the April brook deep in its hollow.
> Cooled by the night the odors that the horses had left
>   behind were in her nostrils . . .

The dark strength of the stallion had heard her com-
　　ing; she heard him
Blow the shining air out of his nostrils, she saw him
　　in the white lake of moonlight
Move like a lion along the timbers of the fence;
He drew away from it, the hooves making soft thun-
　　der in the trodden soil.

And this vivid picture of the sport of the sea-lions:

　　　　　　　　　　and the crying of the sea-lions far
　　down below,
Where eight or ten were lying in a circle by the softly
　　heaving kelp-bed, as their custom is, and gazed
With great mild eyes at the sky and the night of water.
　　Then they sing in their manner, lifting up sleek
Dark-shining muzzles to the white moon, making a
　　watery noise of roaring and a lonely crying
For joy of life and the night.

Other beautiful and original passages on nature and
natural objects are the following:

O shining of night, O eloquence of silence, the mother
　　of the stars, the beauty beyond beauty,
The sea that the stars and the sea and the mountain
　　bones of the earth and men's souls are the foam
　　on, the opening
Of the womb of that ocean.

And this passage about rain:

The gray mothers of rain sail and glide over,
The rain has fallen, the deep-wombed earth is re-
　　newed;

Under the greening of the hills
Gulls flock in the black furrows.

And this:

the mountain, but dimly
To be seen through leaning pillars of rain.

And this about clouds:

the brave clouds with flashing bellies
Crossing the gorge like a fleet of salmon.

One of the most beautiful of Jeffers longer nature
poems is *Fauna*. It intoxicates like the ripe wine of
California's grapes, and is an ardent celebration of the
eternal, feminine warmth of the living earth:

Because the mouth that kissed her body brown
Was not a man's but a great God's the Sun's.
There Nais we snared her once
In the fragrance of the grapes, where she fell down
By the winepress on the heap of hulls and stones.

*   *   *   *   *   *   *

And here gathered
Arab frankincense buds and Syrian myrrh,
With mazy seaflowers that the seafoam fathered
In warm live waters south the Hydaspian gulf,
They fell like snowflakes from the flaming air,
And frightened by the wonder Fauna's wolf
That still had watched, ran off. From the upper Nile
Came lotuses, and laurels from Lesbos isle.
Great lilies from large Asia congregated
Amazed the tolerant vintage-month with massed

Mounds of May sweet; the vast
Sky-heads of the earth-out-of-mind Himalaya mated
Their snow-buds with starved bloom Siberia cast.

And soon came homelier and more kindly blossoms,
Orchids from under Araucanian Andes
Were forced into the beauty of Fauna's bosoms,
Through her good sleep, where the crushed grapes
    had lain,
But maidenly in the opening of her hand is
A white globe-tulip fainting without stain,
Fed from peninsular forests of Monterey,
And at her feet white flagflowers fainted away,
The Santa Cruz wood-irises; and brown

As her sunned body and excellent as her mouth
Was mingled a new growth,
Bronze-bells of redwood darknesses that drown
The Santa Lucian Rivers of the South.

While hermit yuccas from La Cumbre wasted
Flaked petal-wealth and faint white fragrance there,
Young sand-verbena from south shores was tasted
Intense among the perfumes, native poppies
Paled in the splendor of the spun-gold hair,
Wild yellow violets of the liveoak coppice
Flowered up through all, strange-shapen and blood-
    red
Were phallic snowplants on the perfumed bed

Strown for a laughing symbol; from the south
They also, from the firforest that grows
About Bear Lake or close
Under cold Grayback; and with that uncouth
Male flower mated the moist and female rose.

We moderns must take down and search through our dusty volumes of Wordsworth, Keats and Clare to find such an "all-embracing sensuousness," projections "behind the superb, sufficient forehead of nature" such as Jeffers has seen, touched and presented for our pleasure and consideration. Far too long have we drifted, and we wonder at ourselves that we have been inveigled into giving some attention to the "tentative movements" and "uncertain waverings" of the Cummingses, Doolittles and Pounds. Remember that it happened "when we were very young." Now we have grown, we may be forgiven and they forgotten.

Jeffers's nature poetry holds the senses in a direct spiritual experience. While reading it we never ask ourselves what is the meaning of life. We look at the grass, the trees, the ever-changing sky through the windows of trains, automobiles, skyscraper offices or city apartments; but we no longer live with these unnatural phenomena. With Jeffers we see things in an Edenic state: God walks in the cool of the morning with Adam and Eve among the first flowers, beasts and birds. With him we have

> entered the life of the great forest
> And the great life of ancient peaks, the patience of
>   stone.
> I felt the changes in the veins
> In the throat of the mountain, a grain in many cen-
>   turies, we have our own time, not yours; and I
>   was the stream

Draining the mountain wood; and I the stag drink-
   ing; and I was the stars
Boiling with light, wandering alone, each one lord of
   his own summit; and I was the darkness
Outside the stars, I included them, they were a part
   of me.
I was mankind also, a moving lichen
On the cheek of the round stone . . . they have not
   made words for it, to go behind things, beyond
   hours and ages,
And be all things in all time, in their returns and
   passages, in the motionless and timeless center,
In the white of the fire, how can I express the excel-
   lence I have found, that has no color but clearness,
No honey but ecstasy.

Before concluding this approach to the work of Jeffers, let us try to indicate his rightful place in present-
day literature, and also to guess his position in the future of American poetry, by an act of what Powys calls
"imaginative will". This, he tells us, will give us "the
power to treat" our poet "in his lifetime as though he
were dead, which is the supreme triumph over matter
of the human spirit." Whitman's *Leaves of Grass*
shocked the American gentleman of his generation.
"The gentleman who directs his skill to those arts
which raise the polished man above the barbarian" was
disappearing with the evolutionary period and cosmic
philosophy started by John Fiske. Whitman, "hanker-
ing, gross, mystical, nude," stepped into the poetic

arena with the popular and beloved Longfellow, whose "escape" poem, Hiawatha, appeared the same year as *Leaves of Grass.* In spite of Whitman's simple universality and complex cosmic spirit, we find many of the sentimental, almost imperialistic views of the nation scattered like so many seeds among the "Leaves." Many of them echo Lincoln's "we are indeed the treasury of the world," or "this nation should be on the Lord's side."

We must admit that Whitman, like other original poets, had his limitations. He had not, though he believed he had, the power to reach the average man through his poetry. If he ever reached him, he reached him directly, personally and not through or with his poetry. When Whitman forgets the "average man" and frees himself from his mania for cataloging "democratic art" and popularizing sex facts, when he obeys his "essential, ultimate me," he could write a *Passage to India, The Sleepers, Chanting the Square Deific* and such lines of rational mysticism as we find in the very first edition of the *Leaves:*

> Rise after rise bow the phantoms behind me,
> Afar down I see the huge Nothing—the vapour from the
> Nostrils of Death—I know I was even there,
> I waited unseen and always, and slept while God carried me through the lethargic mist,
> And took my time, and took no hurt from the fetid carbon.

This fragment proves what Whitman had in mind when he wrote that real poetry "must possess a certain fluid, aerial character, akin to space itself, obscure to those of little or no imagination, but indispensable to the highest purposes."

Thus Whitman, the cosmic poet will always remain the divine property of the ages and not the poet of the "average man" in a "successful Democracy" of America.

Today Michell Roberts, one from the "engineering school" of the newer English poets among whom Auden, Botrall, Lehman, Lewis, Spender and Warner are the leaders, writes: "At least these poets (including himself) are trying to bring poetry back into the life of the common man."

If they do find understanding readers among common men they have accomplished nothing less than a miracle.

On the other hand, our American proletariat poets Rolfe, Gessner, Spector, Kalar, and others who are gathering strength from the life of the daily worker seem to be nearer in reaching the common man than our Oxford graduates of "the engineering school." Let us take a sample from Auden as the kind of poetry Roberts thinks reaches the common man:—

"Me, March, you do with your movements master and
    rock
With wing-whirl, whale-wallow, silent budding of cell;
Like a sea-god the communist orator lands at the pier:
But, O, my magnet, my pomp, my beauty

More tolling to heart than the sea
Than Europe or my own home town
Today is parted from me
And I stand on our world alone."

This class-conscious, but highly artificial bit of verse
seems far from bare simplicity.

We might accept their work "in its present semi-
private" condition as their way of looking at the present
world change.

We believe they

"wish to be plain spoken,
    want their voices to expand,
We will our voices to fly out as fruit,
Their meaning luscious, digestible; nor rind;
Spit out the seeds to sprout, if they're a mind,
And if they don't, so what?"

writes L. Kirstein.

The optimistic idealization of humanity spread far
and wide during the eighteenth and early part of the
nineteenth centuries. It made of democracy a new religion, much as communism is held today in Russia.
In his preface to the first edition of the *Leaves* Whitman writes: "The United States themselves are essentially the greatest poem," and "America is the race of
races." He called the then growing New York "a city
of the world"; he writes, "I hear America sing for you,
Democracy," and "I dreamed in a dream." We see
why, from the year 1855, the cry of America has been

for a "will to power"—power of the "materialized" class, the mass-minded, who consciously seek selfish ends with their democratic "equality of man" slogans. This demoralizing class, to be found in all epochs of our civilization, is the class which, as Matthew Arnold pointed out, "always materializes the upper classes, vulgarizes the middle, and brutalizes the lower classes." Whitman, being a child of his generation, did not see that our "democratization" would begin our demoralization. Our present-day poets, Carl Sandburg and Edgar Lee Masters and the late Vachel Lindsay, have all sung the typical hundred per cent Americanism. Edwin Arlington Robinson sings of our decadent city life, Frost of decadent New England farmers, but Jeffers of the decadent continent of America. We see why Plato excluded poets from his Republic—they belong to the "politics of eternity."

To Jeffers the dream cities of Whitman's democracy have become the cities of Thompson's "dreadful night." Machine noises, smoke, sounds out of underground darkness, out of the dusty air, all breeding weariness of life—these to Jeffers are like a cloud of murderous gas stealing upon humanity—humanity caught in a trap, "the trap that catches noblest spirits" —all indications of the downfall of a "perishing republic" thirsting for more sacrifice in a new world war. Today Engle, an adolescent good will poet, sings again "the unique American dream" and "the old American courage" under the New Deal plan. He finds America a land of youth, hope and God's plenty. We must take him with perceived sense of irony and not superiority. Overwhelming occurrences might happen when winter comes and spring is far behind. As for the present, we may dismiss him with the words of W. H. Auden:

> He knows not if it be seed in time to display
> Luxuriantly in a wonderful fructification
> Or whether it be but a degenerate remnant
> Of something immense in the past but now
> Surviving only as the infectiousness of disease.

Thus we see Jeffers as a poet of transition "between two worlds, one dead (or dying), the other powerless to be born." The ideals in art, literature and poetry that prevailed a generation ago are a part of the history of mankind in a process of reaction. The poets among the economists and politicians have also had their say in their lifetime. We admit that these forces—the forces of mechanistic and revolutionary evolutions—will never reach a state of rest. Each individual life is a fragment of this vital life-force within the cosmos throughout all eternity. This eternal repetition—Bergson's *evolution créatrice*—may drive mad a Pascal or a Nietzsche; nevertheless it moves us on. Each epoch of civilization cries to the poet *"Cantate mihi canticum novum."* In his book, *Sketches in Criticism*, Van Wyck Brooks writes: "We have surely had too many facile meliorists, too many apostles of the glad hand. How much we should enjoy the spectacle of a sour-faced American

Schopenhauer, an indigestible American Tolstoy, an insufferable American Ibsen, an incredible American Nietzsche—just one true-blue, solitary rhinoceros." And, lo and behold! here is this one, solitary, pessimistic poet of our Tartarian darknesses, Robinson Jeffers.

Our "perishing republic" is fortunate in having such wide-awake, understanding critics as Wilson, Krutch, Brooks and Mumford, to stand against the mere "debunkers," those detergent critics who represent the "blind mouths" of the intellectually inclined Babbitts and the communists.

There is another poet, almost unknown to the wider American public, who, like Jeffers, is American-born, and who, in his own way, sees us as does Jeffers. He, too, in his two volumes of published work, has uttered a protest against present-day American life. This poet is E. Merrill Root, whom Frost has declared to be "the best young poetic prospect in the country." Mystic and rebel, Root sees that

> Calvary is continent
> To-day. America
> Is but a vast and terrible
> New Golgotha.

and

> I know too well, America,
> How reckless, cruel, lovable, heterodox,
> The river of your blood's Niagara

Roars down magnificent—upon the rocks.
Yet I see also—past the ape's dull night—
Prometheus, and the dreadful morning's light!

So he calls

both for myself and earth
Upon the lightning for deliverance—
Out of the world's grey clouds in golden birth
The spirit's flame and noble arrogance.

The basic reality of Root's "inner light" is the Sun who writes on our wall

The ancient poetry of Day
In his gigantic scrawl

Root distrusts the modern process of poetry defined by Ezra Pound as "inspired mathematics." To Root, reason is only a candle that

lights a little room:
I see its universe as neat and scant
And cozily lighted. Meanwhile over me
Vast suns go roaring thru immortal gloom.

Root like Jeffers uses the world-old symbols which give simplicity and suggestive power to their verse, the "healthy speech" quality Thoreau above all else sought in poetry.

This poet, too, feels that "at the fall of an age men must make sacrifice to renew beauty, to restore strength." If by genius we mean "the age-long miracle of man's creation of beauty out of utility; meaning out of chaos, permanence in the midst of a world of flux," then both Root and Jeffers have surely answered "the human question," which is at present an episodic, not an epic, question.

In the work of Stephen Spender, an English poet, we see a strong resemblance to Jeffers and Root, particularly in their poetic self-annihilation in the interests of attaining a higher plane of creative imagination.

As Spender himself says, his spirit "has learned to lean outward for seeing." He possesses the impulse of a definite orientation toward living truths he has experienced, and therefore comes very near Jeffers when he writes:

> Different living is not living in different places
> But creating in the mind a map
> Creating in the mind a desert
> An isolated mountain or a kinder health-resort.

This turning away and creating in the mind an isolated mountain means turning to the center of one's being and finding there the fountain of life for creative energy. He writes further:

> This century chokes me under roots of night
> I suffer like history in Dark Ages where
> Truth lies in dungeons . . .

This proclaims his belief that our age is one of renaissance. He thinks continually

of those who were truly great
Who, from the womb, remembered the soul's history
Through corridors of light where the hours are suns,
Endless and singing.

"Town-bred" like Jeffers, he feels "the roots of each earth-cry tear me apart." Philosophically, he feels that he is "never being, but always at the edge of Being," that is, that man is in a continual process of overcoming self, growing, transforming his will to a more and more individualistic expression in spite of the materialistic collectivism that tends to wipe out spiritual growth. We learn that Spender has been "under the shadow of war," and now has reached a stage in which "the city builds its horror in my brain, this writing is my only wings away" from this day, a "time when grief pours freezing over us, when the hard light of pain gleams at every street corner" where he has observed "cripples pass with limbs shaped like questions in their odd twist." He has

                      expected always
        Some brightness to hold in trust,
        Some final innocence
        To save from dust;
        That, hanging solid
        Would dangle through all
        Like a created poem
        Or the dazzling crystal.

These lines are strikingly like Jeffers in their pessimistic outlook and tragic sense of life, yet he is not a mere tyro nor imitator of Jeffers. Compare also the following:

> Lives risen a moment, joined or separate,
> Fall heavily, then are always separate,
> A stratum unreckoned by geologists,
> Sod lifted, turned, slapped back again with spade.

No wonder English critics and his fellow poets have compared Spender to Shelley and the later Greek lyricists. Of all modern British poets, Spender sees' most definitely that, in our perishing old-world empires, "prosperity is founded on the agonies of the past." To Root, Spender and Jeffers, this age has become the *taedium vitae* of the spirit. They consider the subjection of the individual to the externalizing, mechanizing collective influences of the age as weakening and pernicious to the modern psyche. If culture is concerned with the values by which we live, and these values are grounded in our poets' reactions to or criticism of life, then Spender's as yet still, small voice in England responds, too, with Jeffers and Root, to this realistic phase in modern poetry—a phase beyond the objectivists and mere singers of an empty day. In him too we sense the realization that we are living at the end of an epoch, in a period of transition, and that the rhythm of poetic art is changing with it. This change in poetical standards leans toward a catastrophic, generative activity in verse itself. It is incredibly surprising that Spender and Auden have found an enthusiastic reception among the esoterically inclined communists. They seem to read much about the "strength of proletariat" art between the lines of these poets that is hidden to the uninitiated and to the mass of poetry readers in general. "Most critics" wrote Pope

> fond of some subservient art
> Still make the whole depend upon a part.

With due respect to the hidden political ideals, Spender's and Auden's work must be judged by standards of the modern temper in the arts, and not by propaganda for causes in the making.

If the poet becomes a tool, sling, sword or any other thing for pure propaganda work, he becomes tragicomic. "We laugh" says Bergson "every time a person gives us the impression of being a thing." And we laugh at our president's campaign antics and slogans, we laugh at the Elmer Gantrys, Isadora Duncan's late Victorian falsifications of the Greek temperament, at Harry Crosby's erotic ejaculations, and O'Neill's latest dry-as-dust masked rehearsals.

It is tragic laughter because we miss the sincerity of natural feelings in these mechanical actions and reactions in the things we laugh at. It is the tragic laughter of a Daumier or a Goya which we sense in W. H. Auden, a contemporary of Spender. His cursory *Paid on Both Sides* and the cynical *Dance of Death* are both the sophisticated laughter of a class-conscious intellectual, who recognizes the passing of the capitalistic order of things in our changing civilization.

In Jeffers we hear the tragic laughter in the "hard brought up" Cawdor, before he blinds himself:

> Blue-kingfisher laughing, laughing in the lit boughs
> Over lonely water,
> Is there no man not duped and therefore you are
>   laughing?
> No strength of a man
> But falls on folly before it droops into dust?
> Go wicked arrow down the ocean
> And learn of gulls: they laugh in the cloud, they
>   lament also.
> The man who'd not be seduced, not in hot youth,
> By the angel of fools, million-worshiped success,
> The self-included man, the self-armored,
> And never beguiled as to a bull nor a horse,
> Now in his cooled and craglike years
> Has humbled himself to beg pleasure: even power was
>   better.
> Laugh kingfisher, laugh, that is their fashion.
> Whoever has discerned the vanity of water will desire
>   wind.

The uprooted soil of modern poetry is characterized not as a refuge, but as an attack at the wastelanders now driven by their trades into "a sleepy corner." The negative verbalisms of the anti-poetic minded M. Moore, Pond, and Stevens are slowly becoming the *complexio oppositorum* to the newer spirits in modern history. We have a definite feeling that the very recent experiments in poetic form are a part of the breaking away or rather, inbreak of a poetic renascence. The poet of the near "opening age" must be a modernist and, in a certain sense, a primitivist. By primitivism we mean a "positive spiritual impulse," to borrow Lewis Mumford words.

No doubt Seneca living on the verge of the economic as well as the cultural decline of the Roman Empire had "cultural primitivism" in mind when he said *"simplici cura constant necessaria: in delicias laboratur."*

Seneca's *necessaria* is what Jeffers calls the "permanent things" in his poetry and

> While this America settles in the mould of its vulgarity heavily thickening to empire

protest against collective mechanisation becomes

> only a bubble in the molten mass, pops and sighs out and the mass hardens

and accepts the perishing empire's industrialized vulgarity-luxury for a shining democracy.

In connection with neo-primitivism we might consider Jesse Stuart, our Kentucky farmer-poet, who has delivered himself of seven hundred and three sonnets under the title "Man with a Bull-Tongue Plow." We could call him the *sensus communis;* the commonsense faculty in modern poetry. He feels the earth physically and expresses what Croce calls "the primitive barbarism of sensation" lustily in his ruggedly rhymed verse:

> "For I can live—to hell with all your gold,
> I know I'm strong enough to work the soil."

and

> "if one hears gods on the wind and prays
> And sees white islands float across the sky
> Then this one has a poet's moods and ways
> And not the little ways of those that cry
> To God from corners on the dirty street
> Expecting money from the passers-by."

Stuart believes that the man who draws joy from the poetic feeling is a true poet, though he has never written a verse all his life. And with John Clare he loves

> the verse that mild and bland
> Breathes of green fields and open sky.

Croce gives us the historical, sociological and philosophical ground which accounts for our return to the primitive which he attributes to Vico's law of "reflux": "The mind, after traversing its course of progress, after rising from sensation successively to the imaginative and rational universal and from violence to equity, is bound in conformity with its eternal nature to retraverse the course, to relapse into violence and sensation, and thence to renew its upward movement, to commence a reflux."

The new poets must realize that the real essence of poetry is not so much in the actual word but in the thought that precedes the word, thus revealing the meaning of the Platonic λόγος in their poetic art.

> It's not the purpose o'poetry to sing
> The beauty o' the dirt frae which we spring
> But to cairry us as faur as ever it can
> 'Yont nature and the Common Man

For

> a poet maun see in a thing
> Ev'n what looks trumpery or horrid,
> A subject equal to ony
> —A star for the forehead!

The above are examples of the poetic consciousness we have in mind from the little known Scotch poet, Hugh M'Diarmid, who envisages in his verse the birth of a new mystic conciliation:

> A sudden thought of God
> Came like a wind
> Ever and again
> Rippling them as waters over stars.

As with many of our poetic minds, M'Diarmid too realizes that

> The agony has lasted far too long,
> It is beyond us—this anachronism
> Of false love spawning out of habit,
> And claiming as its rights the wrongs it does

As to the failure of spiritual progress he feels very
much like Jeffers:

> Progress?—There is nae progress; nor shall be,
> The cleverest men aye find out again
> For foolish mobs that follow to forget,
> As in the Past

We sense a two-directional ratiocination in M'Diarmid's
most ambitious, long poem "*To Circumjack Cencrastus, or The Curly Snake*." Cencrastus symbolizes
the spirit of cosmic energy that is at the root of all life:

> There is nae movement in the warld like yours
> Save faith's

In the heterogeneous mixture of unevenly balanced and
varied meters, a very strong Scotch vernacular and
literary gallimaufry, unexpectedly we come across
lines which place the volume among the notable con-
tributions to modern poetry in general.

M'Diarmid's poems are filled with visions and flashes
of immediate insight which for instance a Burns could
never see, for Burns lacked what M'Diarmid terms
the "frichtfu' sensation o' seein.'"

In its disjointed tectonics the Curly Snake resembles
Humbert Wolf's *The Uncelestial City*, at once revolutionary and conservative in its presentation of contemporary facts and poetic fancy.

In the work of both these poets we miss a full realization of concentration and in its place we get frag-

ments of expedient perception. We feel M'Diarmid is working out a new "revolutionary art form" of which the Soviet poet Vladimir Maiakovski is reported to have said: "We have now swept away the dust of verbal antiquity and shall only make use of fragments." With Jeffers M'Diarmid is in opposition to Lenin's dream of "an electrified earth" and the soviet futurist critics who "behold the insignificance" of a Dostoevsky, Shelley or Blake "from the top of a skyscraper".

With M'Diarmid as with Jeffers the principal question of art is not art for art's sake, nor art for propaganda's sake, but the vital question

> "is frae hoo deep
> A life it springs—and syne hoo faur
> Up frae's it has the poo'er to leap

M'Diarmid encounters the same fundamental truths as Jeffers by showing the paralogisms of materialistic communism and how incapable it is to save human societies by material process alone:

> I'm oot for shorter hours and higher pay
> And better conditions for a' workin' folk
> But ken the hellish state in which they live's
> Due maistly to their ain mob cowardice.
> Yet tho' a' men were millionaires the morn
>   As they could easily be
> They'd be nae better than maist rich folk noo
> And nocht that maitters much 'ud be improved
>   And micht be waur.

The faith of our future poets is strikingly exemplified in the words of Ronald Bottrall, another English poet who is loosening himself from the dominant forces of the wastelanders and taking root in a new "unfooted ploughland" of his own:—

> There is yet time, even though the clock
> Is set, there is yet time to brave
> The annals of our age, to put our "wave
> Of progress" in the proper place, recant
> Our late betrayal and plant
> Within the shadow of the rock . . .

Our modern poets, except Jeffers, lack the totality of a realized selfhood; with most of them the self and the not-self are still in a disunited state of becoming. This is one of the reasons why so many of them are incapable of creating harmonious, if not perfect or permanent works of art.

Bottrall realizes this state of consciousness:

> We are dismembered
> Into myriad broken shadows
> Each to himself reflected in a splinter of that glass
> Which once we knew as Cosmos.

We know Keats held a similar view by his saying that "the poetical nature has no self—it is everything and nothing." A realized selfhood, emanating perhaps from ancient minds, ancient traditions and cultures, is precisely what Jeffers has regenerated in *The Tower*

Beyond Tragedy. It should be accepted as the first, direct, harmonious modern work of poetic art equal to the Greeks. In *The Tower Beyond Tragedy* we find what Hegel calls "concreate unity" of a mind where intelligence "is at once self-collected in this externally existing material, and yet in this self-collectedness sunk in the outselfness."

Stark Young has summarized as follows this change in the modern poetic spirit: "The human spirit triumphs over the past when it destroys whatever in the past has grown dead, and now denies life. The human spirit can triumph also over the present, destroying it in things dead, but preserving from or drawing on the past for what is alive there."

Out of centuries of meditations this spirit brings to Jeffers, the poet, "remembrance of things past," and he builds conclusions thereon:

> I have come home to myself, behold me.
> I bruised myself in the flint mortar and burnt me
> In the red shell. I tortured myself, I flew forth,
> Stood naked of myself and broke into fragments,
> And here am I moving the stars that are me.
> I have seen these ways of God: I know no reason
> For fire and change and torture and the old returnings.
> He being sufficient might be still: I think they admit
>   no reason: they are the ways of my love.
> Unmeasured power, incredible passion, enormous
>   craft: no thought but burns darkly
> Smothered with its own smoke in the human brain-

> vault: no thought outside a certain measure in
> phenomena:
> The fountains of the boiling stars, the flowers on the
> foreland, the ever-returning roses of dawn . . . .

Archibald MacLeish, the abstract objectivist and a far superior poet, for instance to Williams Carlos Williams, and a little below Hart Crane, in his poem *Ars Poetica* says:

> A poem should be palpable and mute
> As a globed fruit . . . .
> A poem should not mean
> But be (conclusive enough)

Those of us to whom art-for-art's sake, or poetry as "abstract art" is anathema, will resent this statement. We may divorce art from ethics, utilitarianism and politics, but in no way can we conceive that all poetry is a meaningless, moveless object in itself, devoid of all verisimilitude.

It is surprising to hear Baudelaire, the neotheric among the budding "verbo-motor" reactionists and art-for-art's sake proselytes, write:—

"The puerile art-for-art's theory by its exclusion of all ethics, and often even passion, was of necessity sterile. It puts itself into flagrant contradiction with all the spirit of humanity. In the name of the higher principles which constitute universal life we have the right to declare its quality of heterodoxy."

Speaking of his own poetry he declares that it is "deep and complex, bitter and coldly diabolical" and that it will not "appeal to the eternally frivolous."

If the destiny of our modern poetry is to rouse and realize itself as a new and fresh organism toward a future prepossession, a "planting between tonight and tomorrow" in Jeffers's words, then its makers cannot return to the "gaudy and inane phraseology" Edmund Spencer complained against in his day.

It is as difficult to dissociate Dante from his fight against the corruption of mediaeval Italy or Whitman from his scorn of American Puritanism as it is to picture Jeffers other than warring against American materialism. Perhaps, as was the case with the other two, the vision in Jeffers's poetry will be comprehended more fully in the future, when the present-day economic struggle in which the whole world is involved has ended. Perhaps at some time far in the future self-interest, greed for wealth, lust of war, will have been conquered. When men shall see the fallacy of thinking *en masse* and become capable of thinking individually, inwardly out, realizing the unity between the self and the cosmic not-self, then the most vital of all human questions may be answered, the highest aim of civilization reached. Perhaps this is what Christ meant by saying, "Men do not live by bread alone," and Socrates by his magical word, σωφροσύνη. We are living in an age of experimentation; many of us know that no communist's dream of machine-power can ever restore the world to an order that will satisfy the deeper hopes of humankind nor liberate it. "For we are not dogs to be satisfied when a few bones are flung to us, though they be automobiles and subways, electric lights and airplanes. There is something else in us that makes the very essence of our humanity; we have to live *for* something. The deepest hell that some of us could ever fall into would be to have everything to live with and nothing to live for. . . . "

Jeffers shows that, no matter what man has done toward subduing nature, he has not subdued himself. He is still the brute—blind, instinctive, naked, savage, in spite of his claims to scientific knowledge, religious beliefs, and the polish of education. Even our President in his inaugural address emphasized the fact that "only a foolish optimist can deny the dark realities of the moment."

John Strachey, the most intellectual and cultural of all the critics and theorists of communism, despite his optimistic guesses senses the tragic element: "Nor, of course, will the coming of fully developed communism itself, solve all our problems. For example, the supreme enemy of man's complacency, his knowledge of his own proximate annihilation by death, must long remain with him under any system of society."

Since Nietzsche looked upon tragedy as an embodiment of dream figures symbolizing the eternal realities of human life with its suffering, loss and pain inherent in some early existence, it is to him the product of the

Protean conflict between Dionysus, the youthful god of
nature and sex, and Apollo, the god of lyric poetry and
culture.

One critic of Jeffers laments that he "has no message
and no solace" for the modern man. Is it not rather
outside the modern temper to ask or hope for a message
from our poets? The Victorians were in the habit of
asking for messages from their poets—and some of
those that were given were pointless. That a poet's
perceptions have no place in a scientifically governed
life-scheme we, like Plato, take for granted. What has
value for us is the poet's *attitude* toward our scientific
or political systems. Jeffers's opinion of science, from
one point of view, at least, is clear in the following
lines:

> Science, that makes wheels turn, cities grow,
> Moribund people live on, playthings increase,
> But has fallen from hope to confusion at her own
>   business
> Of understanding the nature of things.

Thus the greatest poetic consciousness of our day
sums up the scientific question. The man who demands a reality more solid than that of the poetic
consciousness knows not what he seeks in poetry. He
knows not that "the substance of poetry is spiritual
experience communicated as representative of the
nature of man." The mystic poets of all ages have
dwelt in a universe richer and more terrible than ours;

they ride, on Master Eckhart's swift steed, through suffering that bears them to perfection, through renunciation, to reach at last that supreme summit attainable in earthly existence, that one solace of all great poets—spiritual exaltation of the individual. This exalted state, inexplicable in terms of reason, is the height upon which intelligence reaches concrete unity in "self-collectedness" and in "out-of-selfness."

Yet after all we can receive from our poets only as much as we ourselves are capable of giving to the comprehension of their work; we recognize their Promethean-bound universe and find the understanding of their attitudes conditioned by the mental reactions of our own psyches. Keats wrote in one of his letters: "I am certain of nothing but the holiness of the heart's affections and the *truth of the imagination*." Even that highly polished pillar of the Victorian Age, Lord Tennyson, knew that "our little systems have their day . . . and cease to be."

No poet, philosopher nor scientist can prove the existence of anything outside his own thoughts, the natural forces of his own desires and unidealized impulses; all he can feel is a cosmic, harmonious faith in Reality or Truth. Poetry and art in general are not revelations of actuality; the values that the productive imagination of the poet attributes to nature, love or death are not to be found in biological studies of nature or man, nor in handbooks of psychoanalysis. The poet has always remained, remains, and will ever remain outside the systematic limitations of face and science.

In his *Religio Poetae* Coventry Patmore says: "The most peculiar and characteristic mark of genius is insight into subjects which are dark to the ordinary vision and for which ordinary language has no adequate expression." To demanders of messages Jeffers understandingly replies:

> It is hard for men to stand by themselves,
> They must hang onto Marx or Christ or mere progress.
> Clearly it is hard.

or

> After all, after all we endured, who has grown wise?
> We take our mortal momentary hour
> With too much gesture, the derisive skies
> Twinkle against our wrongs, our rights, our power.

To illustrate this rather paradoxical truth, let us consider the two most popular poets of the new Russia and their poems with a propaganda message. Block in *The Twelve* and Byely in *Christ Arisen* use the figure of Christ and not that of Lenin or Marx to lead the revolutionary parade. In fact, both these poets find it hard to "hang on to" Christ—but they do hang on to him—and why? The today somewhat ambiguous figure of Jesus can easily be made an objectified symbol for inciting war or restoring peace. Extreme opposites can meet in this universally accepted symbol of the tragic consciousness of humanity. The illusory

and the eternal are the hardest illusions for humanity
to break away from; it is the everlasting parable of the
wheat and the tares. The moderns hate it, but they
still hang on to the figure of the Christ in spite of
change and the higher criticism:

> the mind smiles at its own rebellions,
> Knowing all the while that civilization and the other
>   evils
> That make humanity ridiculous, remain
> Beautiful in the whole fabric, excesses that balance
>   each other
> Like the paired wings of a flying bird . . .
>
> The same-colored wings of imagination that the crowd
>   clips, in lonely places newgrown.

Let us complete a picture of Jeffers by likening him
to one gifted like Apollo with "that freedom from the
wilder emotions, that philosophical calmness of the
sculptor-god. His eye must be sun-like according to its
origin, even when it is angry and looks displeased."

But in his work, in his tragedies and his prelogical
nature poems and lyrics, he has shown himself to us
under the charm of a Dionysus "incited to the highest
exaltation of all his symbolic faculties; something never
before experienced struggles for utterance, the annihilation of the veil of Maya . . ."

For the moment let us accept the poet Jeffers as a
pilgrim of eternity passing through our planet with

gifts of beauty enabling us to sing "we also have known beauty"—

Divinely superfluous beauty
Rules the games, presides over destinies, makes trees
    grow
And hills tower, waves fall.
The incredible beauty of joy
Stars with fire the joining of lips,
O let our loves too
Be joined, there is not a maiden
Burns and thirsts for love
More than my blood for you, by the shore of seals
    while the wings
Weave like a web in the air
Divinely superfluous beauty.

PART VI

BIBLIOGRAPHY

BIBLIOGRAPHY

Writings

Flagons and Apples. Los Angeles: Grafton Publishing Co. 1912.

Mirrors (a short story). The Smart Set, Aug. 1913.

Californians. New York: Macmillan, 1927.

Roan Stallion, Tamar and Other Poems. New York: Boni & Liveright, 1924.

American Poetry, A Miscellany. New York: Harcourt Brace Co. 1927.

The Women at Point Sur. New York: Boni & Liveright, 1927.

George Sterling. Overland Monthly, Nov. 1927.

Cawdor and Other Poems. New York: Horace Liveright, 1928.

Poems. San Francisco: Book Club of California, 1928.

An Artist. Privately printed for John S. Mayfield. Austin, Texas: A. C. Baldwin & Sons, 1928.

Review of Now the Sky and Other Poems, by Mark Van Doren. Books, New York Herald Tribune, Dec. 2, 1928.

Dear Judas. New York: Horace Liveright, 1930.

Descent to the Dead, Poems. New York: Random House, 1932. Limited Edition.

Thurso's Landing and Other Poems. New York: Liveright Inc. 1932.

Give Your Heart to the Hawks and Other Poems. New York: Random House, 1933.

Roan Stallion, Tamar and Other Poems, with a new introduction by the Author. New York. The Modern Library Edition. 1935.

   (containing Poems Reprinted from "A Miscellany of American Poetry," 1927.)

Solstice and Other Poems. New York: Random House, 1935.

Bibliography, Biography and Criticism

Adamic, Louis.   Robinson Jeffers: A Portrait. Seattle: University of Washington Book Store, 1929. University of Washington Chapbook Number 27.

Alberts, S. S.   Bibliography of Robinson Jeffers. New York: Random House, 1933. Limited Edition.

Aiken, Conrad.   Unpacking Hearts with Words. Bookman, Jan. 1929.

Benet, William Rose.   Jeffers Latest Work. Saturday Review of Literature, April 2, 1932.

Bookman, Jan. 1926. A Furious Poet from Pittsburgh. Signed, J. F.

Brown, M. Webster.   Robinson Jeffers: A Poet Who Studied Medicine. Medical Journal and Record, Nov. 6, 1929.

Busch, Niven, Jr.   Duel on a Headland. Saturday Review of Literature, March 9, 1935.

Canby, Henry Seidel.   North of Hollywood. Saturday Review of Literature, Oct. 7, 1933.

Carmelite.   Robinson Jeffers Number, Dec. 12, 1928.

Cestre, C.   Robinson Jeffers. Revue Anglo-Américaine, 1927. Paris.

Daly, James.   Root's Under the Rocks. Poetry, Aug. 1925.

Davis, H. L.   Jeffers Denies Us Twice. Poetry, Feb. 1928.

De Casseres, Benjamin.   Robinson Jeffers: Tragic Terror. Bookman, Nov. 1927.

Dell, Floyd.   Shell-Shock and the Poetry of Robinson Jeffers. Modern Quarterly, Sept.-Dec. 1926.

Deutsch, Babette.   Brains and Lyrics. New Republic, May 27, 1926.

Deutsch, Babette.   Brooding Eagle. New Republic, Jan. 16, 1929.

Deutsch, Babette. Sweet Hemlock. Books, New York Herald-Tribune, Jan. 12, 1930.

Deutsch, Babette. The Hunger for Pain. Books, New York Herald-Tribune, March 27, 1932.

Deutsch, Babette. Comfort in Hell. Books, New York Herald-Tribune, Jan. 31, 1932.

Deutsch, Babette. This Modern Poetry. Chapter VII. N. Y.: W. W. Norton and Co. Inc. 1935.

Deutsch, Babette. In Love with the Universe. Books, New York Herald-Tribune, Oct. 27, 1935.

Gorman, Herbert. Jeffers, Metaphysician. Saturday Review of Literature, Sept. 17, 1927.

Gregory, Horace. Suicide in the Jungle. New Masses, Feb. 13, 1934.

Hale, W. H. Robinson Jeffers: A Lone Titan. Yale Literary Magazine, Dec. 1929.

Hicks, Granville. A Transient Sickness. The Nation, April 13, 1932.

Hutchison, Percy. An Elder Poet and a Young One Greet the New Year. New York Times, Book Review Section, Jan. 3, 1926.

Hutchison, Percy. Sound and Fury in Mr. Jeffers. New York Times, Book Review Section, Oct. 13, 1933.

Hutchison, Percy. Robinson Jeffers Attempts a New Beauty. New York Times, Book Review Section, Sept. 11, 1927.

Hutchison, Percy. Robinson Jeffers Writes Two Passion Plays, New York Times, Book Review Section, Dec. 1, 1929.

Hutchison, Percy. Robinson Jeffers's Dramatic Poem of Spiritual Tragedy, New York Times, Book Review Section, April 3, 1932.

Humphries, Rolfe. Poet or Prophet. New Republic, Jan. 15, 1930.

Humphries, Rolfe. Two Books by Jeffers. Poetry, June, 1932.

Kresensky, Raymond. Fire Burning Cross. Christian Century, June 11, 1930.

Kresensky, Raymond. Beloved Judas. The World Tomorrow, Feb. 1930.

Kreymborg, Alfred. Shine, Perishing Republic. In his *"Our Singing Strength."* New York: Coward-McCann, 1929.

Lehman, Benjamin H. Robinson Jeffers. Saturday Review of Literature, Sept. 5, 1931.

Linn, Robert. Robinson Jeffers and William Faulkner. American Spectator, Nov. 1933.

Mayfield, John S. Robinson Jeffers Receives a Convert. Overland, New Series, Aug., 1928.

Morris, Lawrence S. Robinson Jeffers: Tragedy of a Modern Mystic. New Republic, May 16, 1928.

Morrison, Theodore. Robinson Jeffers. Atlantic Monthly, The Book Shelf. Feb. 1930.

National Enclopedia of American Biography. Robinson Jeffers. Current Volume C, 1930. James T. White & Co. New York.

O'Neill, R. Poetry from Four Men. Outlook, Jan. 16, 1929.

Powell, Lawrence Clark. An Introduction to Robinson Jeffers. Dijon: Imprimérie Berniquad & Privat, 1932.

Rice, Philip Blair. Jeffers and the Tragic Sense. The Nation, Oct. 23, 1935.

Root, E. Merrill. Three Singers Before Sunset. Poetry Folio, Jan.-Feb. 1928.

Rorty, James. In Major Mold. Books, New York Herald Tribune, March 1, 1925.

Rorty, James. Symbolic Melodramas. New Republic, May 18, 1932.

Seaver, Edwin. Robinson Jeffers's Poetry. Saturday Review of Literature, Jan. 16, 1926.

Singleton, Anne. A Major Poet. Books, New York Herald Tribune, Dec. 23, 1928.

Sterling, George. Robinson Jeffers: The Man and the Artist, New York: Boni & Liveright, 1926.

Taggard, Genevieve. The Deliberate Annihilation. Books, New York Herald Tribune, Aug. 28, 1927.

Thompson, Allen Reynolds. The Cult of Cruelty. The Bookman, Jan.-Feb. 1932.

Untermeyer, Louis. Uneasy Death. Saturday Review of Literature, April 19, 1930.

Van Doren, Mark. First Glance (Roan Stallion) Nation, March 11, 1925.

Van Doren, Mark. First Glance (Women at Point Sur) Nation, July 27, 1927.

Van Doren, Mark. Bits of Earth and Water. Nation, Jan. 9, 1929.

Van Doren, Mark. Judas, Savior of Jesus. Nation, Jan. 1, 1930.

Walker, Charles. Women at Point Sur. Independent, Oct. 15, 1927.

Walton, Eda Lou. Dear Judas. The Symposium, Jan., 1930.

Walton, Eda Lou. A Poet at Odds with His Own Civilization. Books, New York Herald Tribune, Oct. 8, 1933.

Winters, Yvor. Robinson Jeffers. Poetry, Feb. 1930.

Zabel, Norton Dauwen. A Prophet in his Wilderness. New Republic, Jan. 1934.